Famous Long Ago

FAMOUS LONG AGO

My Life and Hard Times with Liberation News Service

By Raymond Mungo

Beacon Press Boston

Invocation

"all is vanity
and a striving after wind"

God help us,
refugees in winter dress
skating home on thin ice
from the Apocalypse

—Verandah

*This is dedicated to Marshall Irving Bloom
(1944–1969), who was too good to be also wise.
Some months after I completed this manuscript,
Marshall went to the mountain-top and, saying,
"Now I will end the whole world," left us
confused and angry, lonely and possessed,
inspired and moved but generally broken.*

Contents

Acknowledgments

I should like to thank the following, without whom etc., etc.: my parents, Marshall Bloom, Verandah Porche, Marge Silver, Bob Dylan, Bill Higgs, Max Smith, Blood, Sweat & Tears, Jerry Rubin, Lisbeth Aschenbrenner Meisner, Gaston St-Rouet, Le Duy Van, Wayne Hansen, Laurie Nichols Dodge, The Band, Robert Frost, Harvey Wasserman, Craig Spratt, John Keats, Steve Scolnick, Bob Gross, Tane Yoshida, General Hershey Bar, Mrs. Richards, Eddie Leonard, George Cavalletto, Jeannette Whitmann, Ricardo Stramundo Mungo, Yanooti, Mana, Allen Katzman, the Booger Brothers, Peter Simon, Arlo Guthrie, Pablo Picasso, Nancy Kurshnan, Marty Jezer, Richard Wizansky, Dale Evans, Connie Silver, C. Michael Gies, The Incredible String Band, Mr. LSD, Dick Gregory, Abbie Hoffman, Eldridge Cleaver, Eddie Siegel, Joe Pilati, Steve the Get, Dave Sterrit, Barf-Barf Le Chien, Elliot Blinder, Colonel Packer, Groucho Marx, Dave Dellinger, Barbara Webster, Tom Hayden, Jerry Bruck, LYNDON BAINES JOHNSON, Thomas Loves You, Dick Ochs, the Institute for Policy Studies, Marcus Raskin, Arthur Waskow, Andrew Kopkind, Sue Orrin, Art Grosman and Judy, Dan Riley and Lorna, Jeff Kaliss and Jill, Harry Saxman, Oona Kitoona, Daisy Dawg, Don McLean, Phoebe Snowe, Tom & Alison, Maynard, John Wilton & Lazarus Quan, Marvin Garson, Cathy Hutchison, Steve Marsden, Steve Diamond, Steve Lerner, Steve, the Boston University News, Harold C. Case, Arland Frederick Christ-Janer, Michael Alssid & Rebecca, Robert Sproat, Gerald Fitzgerald and his son Fitzgerald Fitzgerald, Brother Rudolph, Allen Ginsberg, Peter Orlovsky, Gordon Ball, Ethel Merman, John Kaplan, Ellen Snyder, Bill Hunt,

Miss Ketzie, the Baby Farm, the Leyden Commune, Pepper, Brian Keating and Pat, Gulley John, Sarah Mundy, Joan Baez, Pipi LaPeche, Aanu J. Mungo, Jack Smith and Mary Grace, Bill England and Charlotte, Stella, Julian Houston, Susan Levine, Marcia Braun, Stephen Davis, Karens (there are several), Richard M. Schweid, Carol Preis, A. Graham Down, Paul Goodman, Henry David Thoreau, Herman Melville, Richard Rodgers, Ted Kazanoff, Isadora Duncan, Eugene O'Neill, Dan McCauslin, Allen Young, Howard Perdue and Jane, Ken Oleari, Orlando Ortiz, Buzzy and Erica, Gus and Martha, Rodney Parke, Bala-Bala, Abigail Borraem, Marshall Mitnick, Rollie Kowfood, Carl Yastrzemski, Paul Williams, Jimmy Dean, Mel Lyman, Ken Miller's Auction Barn, Oliver Kittoom, Tony Richardson, Miriam Bokser, Brian Kellman, Ronald Jasper, Ethan Allen, Jim Bodge, Amazing Grace Could Save a Wretch Like Me, Bill Kairys and Sue, Male Chauvinism, Jeannette Rankin, J. William Fulbright, Howard Zinn, Murray Levin, Jack Kerouac, Ivan the Czech film-maker, Jesse Kornbluth, Tom Fels, who loaned me money, God bless him, Barbara Garson, who wrote me a poem, Romeo & Juliet, Dave and Marge, Rosemary Goat-Goat, Dolly, the Parallel Pigs, the San Francisco Mime Troupe, Jon Baldoni, Tony Lavorgna, Marine Lieutenant Peter Merry, Agway Outhouse Lime, Peter Lee Gould, Hoppy & Muriel, Roger Blaise, the New England Merchants National Bank, Stève and Janet Marx, Stuart Marx, Karl Marx, and Chico Marx, Tony Gittens, Charlie Leonard and Mimi, Peggy Day, Jon Santlofer and Joi, Richard N. Goodwin, John Roche, the Bugler Tobacco Company, Middle Earth, the San Francisco Oracle, Mildred Loomis and the Green Revolution, Busby Berkeley, Uncle Timothy Leary, Peter Stafford, Dave McReynolds, Arnold Tovell and Joyce, Herbert Marcuse, Douglas Parker, Geoffrey Warner, Robert Williams, Conrad Lynn, Dalton Shipway, Wendell Cox, Walt Disney, the Sierra Club, the Cosmic K, Betty White, and *that's* only the beginning.

Raymond and Marshall before the roof fell in Minneapolis, 1967.

All photographs by Peter Simon

Bala-Bala and Peter Simon in Minneapolis.

Arlington Street Church, Boston, October, 1967.

Verandah Porche.

The Vulgar Marxists and the Virtuous Caucus in their only group photo. See if you can pick out the good guys! New York City, 1968.

The first of May, 1969

Barf-Barf Le Chien.

Michele Clark in Virginia; "We lie down in green pastures."

This is where we live now.

*A portion of Bloom's Band gathers for the aerial photographer
outside their 17-room farmhouse in Montague.*

In wine there is truth.

It's never really the end, even for these guys. That's Richard, Marty, Michele, Raymond, Peter, Verandah, and Laurie, in Vermont, spring of 1968.

My life and hard times

I was born in a howling blizzard in February, 1946, in one of those awful mill towns in eastern Massachusetts, and lived to tell about it. My parents were and are hardworking, ordinary people lacking the "benefits" of higher education and the overwhelming *angst* and cynicism which come with it. I was thus not raised in what most of you would call a middle-class environment, lucky for me. Were I true to my roots I'd now be a laborer in a paper or textile mill, married and the father of two children, a veteran of action in Vietnam, and a reasonably brainwashed communicant in a Roman Catholic, predominantly Irish parish. Instead, I am a lazy good-for-nothing dropout, probably a Communist dupe, and live on a communal farm way, way into the backwoods of Vermont. What went wrong?

At the age of one, I can clearly recall, I was rocked on my mother's lap in the middle of some dark New England winter night; the light from our kitchen lamp shone on the ceiling, and the rocking motion gave it a moving, undulating shape which formed beautiful patterns in my infant mind—obviously the forerunner of the psychedelic experience for me.

At the age of four, I read books—Dick and Jane readers, Bobbsey Twins, Tom Swift, and my parents' encyclopedia of human anatomy, which featured dirty pictures.

At four and one half years, I went to kindergarten, but the girl who sat next to me (her name was Patty) had clammy wet hands and since I was always made to hold her hand during ring-around-the-rosy, I dropped out.

At five and one half, I entered Sister Joseph Antho-

1

ny's first grade classroom and, being physically puny, elected to become the smartest kid in school to compensate. And did.

In the second grade, I was primed for my First Holy Communion. My parents had spent money we couldn't afford on a beautiful white suit in which I was to receive Jesus for the first time. The night before this holy event, I could not sleep, and rose from my bed—over which the picture of Jesus was broadly smiling upon me— to investigate the pantry. There, I ate a whole box of pea- nuts reserved for First Holy Communion festivities the next day; then noticed that it was 3:30 A.M., and realized I had *broken the fast*. (In those days, Catholics were re- quired to fast from midnight on the day they received Communion. To receive the host without having fasted was a mortal sin; that means you go to hell if you suddenly die under the wheels of a runaway car, a tableau which had often been presented to me in Sisters' school.) My al- ternatives were to refuse Holy Communion, thus obeying the sacred law of Rome and disappointing my parents and all my relatives, or else to receive Holy Communion, thus insulting Jesus and Mary but pleasing the family. The pic- ture of Jesus was now crying over my bed. Next morning, I said nothing of the peanuts, just took the First Holy Com- munion, and nobody was the wiser. Except me, I had nightmares of runaway cars and eternal damnation for a year, until I got up the courage to confess the mortal sin to Father Gallivan.

In the eighth grade, puberty came between me and the Church, and I went through a harrowing Stephen Dedalus thing for about three years; you know all about stuff like that so I won't bore you with the details.

For four years, I hitchhiked thirty miles twice a day to attend an R.C. prep school where everybody except me was rich and my tuition was paid by a full scholarship, for I was seen as a promising lad and a likely candidate for the priesthood. I knew the only way out of the mills was through college, so I kept my Stephen Dedalus secrets from everybody until I was safely out of that school with a bundle of college scholarships.

Life began at seventeen. I left home, which was a good and simply virtuous place, and my parents, with whom I have never had a really bad scene, and moved to Boston to get hip about the big big world out there. During my freshman year, I was a violent Marxist, friend of the working class and all that, and relished my background among the oppressed. I was also the victim of a burning need for and involvement with the theatre, having graduated from all the usual precocious-adolescent trips with Romantic poets, Italian composers, Surrealist painters, and dirty novelists. I wrote plays for Theater of the Absurd, which was a big thing back in 1963.

During my sophomore year at college, somebody (God bless him) turned me on to dope. I grew very fond of it, all kinds of it. Dope didn't really become an all-American college preoccupation until 1966 or 1967, so I was a few years ahead in that department. I was then a pacifist and in the process of getting educated about the war in Vietnam, which in 1964 most of my classmates didn't even know was going on. From Vietnam I learned to despise my countrymen, my government, and the entire English-speaking world, with its history of genocide and international conquest. I was a normal kid.

By my junior year, I had lost my virginity and that changed everything. I was living in a wretched Boston slum and working my way through school. I traveled around the country participating in demonstrations against the war in Vietnam, and lived from day to day, smoked a lot of dope and fornicated every night. It was glorious.

In my senior year, I edited the college newspaper and put a lot of stuff about draft resistance, the war, abortions, dope, black people, and academic revolutions in it. Which, even though it was 1966, people seemed to think was pretty far-out stuff indeed. I walked with Mr. LSD and met God, who taught me to flow with it and always seek to be kind. "I am striving to understand."

Toward the very end of my college daze, I had a fat fellowship to Harvard University for graduate school and for lack of anything more exciting to do, intended to use it. But a madman named Marshall Bloom flew into Boston from London one cold April day and put the question to me, did I want to join him in overthrowing the state down in Washington, D.C.? Overthrowing the state seemed to me an excellent idea, it desperately needed to get done, and since if you want something done right you must do it yourself, I said OK why not? Fare thee well simple hometown and good parents, good riddance Catholicism, so long Boston it was nice while it lasted, good-bye school and teachers and warm fat books, I'm off to make my fortune in Washington, D.C., the nation's capital. I'm out to show the emperor without his clothes and tear down the walls of the rotten imperial city and have fun doing it. Fair New England, we'll meet again in the New Age and not before.

That's me on the Merritt Parkway, hauling my cat, her kittens, my friend Steve who turned me on, and all my worldly belongings. There's me on the New Jersey Turnpike puffing on a lighthearted cigarette and leaving behind my debts, hangups, and unborn child. On to Washington to fulfill my years of dreaming of Revolution in my time! Got my manuscripts, my one oil painting, two or three dollars in change, a few records, and my friend. This is the way a young man starts his career.

Now, dear friend, you know as much about me as you need to know. What follows is a story, by no means complete, of what happened to me during the few years after I started. Please don't try to learn anything from it, for there is no message. Try to enjoy it, as I have (at least much of the time) enjoyed putting it down for you. Take it slow, don't try to read it in one sitting, by all means get distracted from time to time. Read it stoned, read it straight, give up and never finish it, it's all the same between friends. Take care of your health and get plenty of rest.

I slept with the Vietcong

Minneapolis, Minnesota, is as bad a place as any to begin. Marshall and I wanted Mrs. Lawrence to fly out there with us; we figured we'd present her as a *happening* along with Krassner, Dick Gregory, and all the underground press freaks. No no no, Mrs. Lawrence protested, she'd stay right here in Washington—"I like the good old *terra firma*, the firma the terra the betta!" Still and all the assembled college newspaper editors of the land were to convene in Minneapolis—God knows why, I wanted it to be in Juneau, Alaska—under the auspices of the United States Student Press Association, that was us. Marshall and I and Bala-Bala ran the Association with as little help as we could manage from Bob Gross, who was the outgoing general-director and now works for *Newsweek*, wouldn't you know. USSPA was one of those bourgey student organizations with a budget in six figures, whose conventions are addressed by senators and executives, hardly the likely group for Marshall Bloom to be head of, but Marshall had edited the *Amherst Student* in his day and I guess he did a good job of it. I had edited the *Boston University News*, the nation's only college paper with its own reportorial staff in Vietnam and its own stoned staff at home—in those days anyway.

It was summer of 1967 and USSPA had to disassociate itself from the National Student Association because *Ramparts* magazine had just divulged that NSA got tons of bread from the CIA; everybody who was anybody was doing his best to disassociate himself from NSA then. So Marshall blew into Washington in July and he persuaded Bob Gross to move USSPA out of the NSA building, for chrissake, and he rented an office building on Church

Street, near Dupont Circle—where the hippies and policemen gather. When I arrived, M and I decided to go one better than that and we published a dirty diatribe against NSA which we distributed at NSA's convention out in College Park, Maryland; for neither of *us* had ever gotten a *cent* out of the CIA and we wanted everybody to know that. We were born too late to even get *solicited* by the CIA. It was all very weird though, for USSPA had always been NSA's brainchild, ward, and mouthpiece—this was in a time when "student organizations" seldom included any real students, it was like any other big business or lobbying outfit, NSA—and we were biting the hand that had fed our predecessors. Shows you what kind of gratitude to expect from kids today.

So we had to go to Minneapolis. Nobody was looking forward to it, but we brought the photographer Peter Simon along just so the trip wouldn't be a total waste; we'd get some good pictures of our crowd out there in the glorious flat Midwest. There was a terrible scene at National Airport which was crowded with soldiers and sailors and millions of frustrated whities trying to split D.C. with their bright green U.S. Treasury checks tucked in breast pockets like hankies. But we finally were off the ground and the plastic stewardess served warmed-over death for brunch as Bala-Bala leaned over to whisper in my ear how she dreamed of someday sleeping with M. It was pretty crazy, as I said.

Minneapolis was worse than I had expected. "Help! I'm nowhere!" I said to myself as I walked the campus of the University of Minnesota looking for a movie theater. I love movies, don't you? The best movie in town was *Darling*, which I had already seen, but I went in anyway and killed a couple of hours that way, but after that I was stuck with only the local 25-cent Boogie Shack for entertainment although Dan Wakefield had thoughtfully brought along some bourbon (he is the author of *Supernation at Peace and War* and other things), so Dan and I got roaring drunk after the marijuana ran out. Our group would do most anything, too, to get away from the assembled college newspaper editors of the land who were a pretty sorry bunch, all hung up on "responsibility" and "accuracy" and "advertising" (though there were exceptions). I suddenly realized why I had never enjoyed being, never quite saw myself as, a college student. Face it, college students as a group are pimply and fatuous and just awful, though as individual persons I guess they are no better or worse than the rest of the planet—which is to say basically worthwhile.

What the assembled college editors did is they fired Marshall because he was a dangerous & irresponsible left-winger and also because they just couldn't understand the words coming out of his mouth. The "issue" was this up-yours-NSA broadside which Marshall had published in the name of USSPA, and the college editors found that unforgivable. They also didn't like his personality or something—remember the days when "popularity" was the highest achievement on campus?—because they were willing to retain *me*, and God knows I was just as dangerous and maybe further to the left. But whereas Marshall will always stick up for his rights and argue with people, etc., my style is to quietly avoid confrontations when I can; I seldom try to convince anybody of anything (except perhaps in print), 'cause if they don't already *know*, I figure I can't tell 'em. If it isn't happening to you right now, I can't save you, brother.

Well, pride being what it is and the United States Student Press Association proving to be so beyond salvation, we had no alternative but to found a competing news service in which we could print anything that came to mind—for indeed there were many publications in 1967 which were years ahead of the *Minnesota Daily*, and who the hell wanted to drag-ass around trying to reform the college press when he could play with such wondrous chums as the *San Francisco Oracle* and Boston's *AVATAR*? We sat around a big table at the University of Minnesota Gymnasium (they still play football there) with the eight or ten college editors who supported Bloom—including the editor from West Point—and an assortment of editors from underground papers whom we'd invited as guests of USSPA, and we plotted the formation of a Resistance Press Service, Rebellious News Agency, Obnoxious Press, or whatever. There was a lot of talk and I couldn't really see it happening, you know, especially since we'd gathered only eighty dollars in starting breads and we were all out of our jobs.

Lots of radicals will give you a very precise line about why their little newspaper or organization was formed and what needs it fulfills and most of that stuff is bullshit, you see—the point is they've got nothing to do and the prospect of holding a straight job is so dreary that they join "the movement" (as it was then called) and start hitting up people for money to live, on the premise that they're involved in critical social change blah blah blah. And it's really better that way, at least for some people, than finishing college and working at dumb jobs for constipated corporations; at least it's not always boring. And that's where we were in Minneapolis, and that's why we decided to start a news service—not because the proliferating underground and radical college press really needed a central information-gathering agency staffed by people they could trust (that was our hype), but because we had nothing else to do. I wasn't going to live in Washington just for the hell of it (& I could easily see that it *would* be hell) and I'd sworn never to return to Boston.

There's M and Bala-Bala and I, ousted & disgraced but on the verge of something, boarding a jet from Minny to Ann Arbor to throw ourselves at the mercy of the *Michigan Daily*'s crazy editor, Roger Rappaport, for a few days of good grass and warm fellowship before returning to the nation's capital, where BB will clean out the Association's stationery supplies and make cocoa in the roachy kitchen. And the phone is always ringing and it's Nick Egelson for me saying c'mon along to Czechoslovakia and we'll live a couple of weeks with the Vietcong. What a story! Boy journalist sleeps with Vietcong! I told Marshall that damn it I had missed a perfectly glorious trip to California (the

Center for the Study of Democratic Institutions was flying me there) onaccounta staying in Minnesota to fight his losing battle and he had better just hand over his last $600 life savings so I could get to Czechoslovakia and by god he did! Kids traveled a lot in those days. Youth fare.

The night before I left for Europe, we three slept all in the one bed and everything was so confused. Were we or were we not going to start a news service? Would BB sleep with M? A fat girl had occupied our basement and given her puppy, cleverly named D.C., an entire room in which to shit on the floor. General Hershey Bar ("Give 'em the navel salute!") was eating mustard sandwiches and drinking lukewarm tea in the living room. I was supposed to go to Europe and make friends there for our new project which still lacked a name, and live with the Vietnamese, and generally carry the ball. Bala-Bala would work up a mailing list and Marshall would go out to Chicago for the New Politics Convention and see who he could hit for some money.

The party of Americans bound for Czechoslovakia were about forty in number and represented every element in what was called the peace and liberation movements, so naturally some of them hated others of them. The conference with the Vietnamese had been arranged by Dave Dellinger to bring the Americans opposed to their government's war together with the victims of it. It was a beautiful idea, it really was. There was another one of those frantic airport scenes; then we all piled into a big KLM and got air-conditioned transit across the great waters and the same old plastic meals. I sat between Thorne Dreyer, the bearded editor of the *Austin Rag*, and Malcolm (*Are You Running With Me, Jesus?*) Boyd, your guerrilla priest, and I got distinctly hostile vibrations from the Dutch stewardess, none of the American school of frigid cordiality.

Planes came down and went up who knows how many times. I vaguely remember Amsterdam and the house in which Anne Frank died; lots of kids on bicycles.

Then there was Vienna and it looked like New York. Then Prague, and Andy (*New Republic, Hard Times*) Kopkind said "Home free!" and Sol (*Ramparts*) Stern laughed. In an effort to avoid the State Department and the *New York Times*, I guess, our conference had been switched from Prague to Bratislava, so we took off again in a seedy two-engine job which served no food; in fact the stewardess got off before takeoff. It was incredibly cold and dark in Bratislava for August and all, but I could dimly make out Uncle Dave getting hugged by Nguyen Minh Vy of the Democratic Republic of Vietnam, and many young couples walking arm in arm on the streets. Gosh.

We were taken to the Dom Rekreachie Hotel, Bratislava's only really twentieth-century-type building—too bad, that; some of the old castles and stuff looked more interesting. You've probably read somewhere else about the charm and warmth of the Vietnamese, well it's all true. Within five minutes I was eating hot dinner with a most wonderful schoolteacher lady who, it turned out, was bearing two hundred pieces of American shrapnel in her body. And I had a very high time with Madame Binh, who later went to the negotiations in Paris, and with a smiling lawyer from Hanoi named Le Duy Van, who absolutely convinced me that the forthcoming news service must become strong and soon speak to *all* the people of America. The people of Vietnam, I learned, are musical and poetic and extraordinarily ready to credit the American public with innocence of the crimes committed against their land, readier than any of *us* were.

We had to say something in response to their overwhelming good cheer, manifestations of brotherhood, gifts, and all, so we talked about our movements back in the U.S. —black power, peace movement, poverty rights organization, draft resistance, student uprisings, etc., etc. One of the last things I'd done in Boston was working with the Draft Resistance Group there so I talked about that, and bam! suddenly I was a heroic young man pitting his life and liberty against the evil Johnson government and while

I sure as hell believe in resisting the draft I didn't feel
especially courageous about it, not considering two hundred pieces of shrapnel. So I was a bit embarrassed.

In the daytime we held these interminable conference sessions with interpreters, maps, films, literature,
speeches, you can see it all, just like the UN; but meals and
special trips were more fun and more revealing. One fine
day we decided to go boating up the Danube (it ain't
blue) to the point where Czechoslovakia meets Yugoslavia,
and then have lunch at a restaurant there. It was fantastic,
like a Renoir painting, just us and the Vietcong, now old
friends enough to ask questions like: do you have a wife?
No, but I have a *woman* (sigh, it was true then). Why do
you always wear dungarees? (I always wore dungarees,
pants and jacket, then.) Well, they're cheap, comfortable,
and durable. Do you still have poets in Hanoi? Yes, but
when the bombs fall they get a little insipid! We spoke in
French—they got it from the French occupation, I got it
from BU.

So to make a long story short the Vietnamese were
a great up in my life, the perfect antidote to the colossal
down I suffered from L. B. Johnson and that crowd. After
we split Bratislava and went to Prague (where I spent
most of my time in the movies and with long-haired incredibly young searchers of freedom who would make a big
stink in 1968 and get rolled by the Russians) I spent several days trying to call Marshall and getting Bala-Bala instead. When I finally did reach M, he was in Denver and I
was standing near a Vietcong friend and we talked about
the news service now in very positive terms, like a fait ac-
compli. But it mustn't be Resistance or Rebellious or Obnoxious Press, said myself, it must be *Liberation* News
Service after, you know, the National Liberation Front.
"That's right," M promptly returned, "because after resistance comes liberation!"

On to Paris for a while. Am I really on the Champs
Élysées, is that the Eyeful Tower? The Tuileries? Movies
weren't a nickel like in Prague, but three dollars like in

New York, and not as good to boot. But I'm here on business let's not forget, don't just enjoy Paris, go organize somebody for Liberation News Service. I decided to organize The Living Theater, which was then in exile at the Place Pigalle. Eric Weinberger and I went over there and rapped with Julian Beck and Judith Malina but we got so stoned that we hardly talked about news at all. Then it was up to the light room for the second "act," the audience having been kept waiting an hour or something. And living all day off the continental breakfast which came with the hotel room in our student/slum neighborhood and getting high off Notre Dame's interior light schemes and so forth.

Then on to London to organize somebody for Liberation News Service. But Harry and Danny, who were Marshall's cronies during the big London School of Economics blowouts, lived right up the hill from a really far-out movie theatre and need I say more? I went down to the *International Times,* London's underground newspaper, but all those people were permanently spaced and didn't seem to distinguish one day from the next, far less political news services from the States. I envied them their freedom.

Can't get a BOAC to Boston, Air France doesn't fly there, gotta take Pan Am even though it's American (read: evil) and when you ask for a cold beer, you'll get a warm Schlitz and pow! you're in Newark right there in the London airport. Nobody believes me when I tell this story but: during the seven-hour flight home, I sat between Tom Lehrer the songwriter, and a businessman member of my local draft board from my hometown, and the rest of the cabin filled with John Kenneth Galbraith and the London cast of *Up With People,* who sang Polly Wolly Doodle All Day and Old Black Joe all the way, accompanied by Lehrer's cutting remarks. My head was spinning by the time Boston came into view.

And afterward the customs guys made me take off all my clothes and rummaged through my things asking like Do You Think a Little Country Like Vietnam Can Beat a Big Country Like Us? and me refusing to answer. They even ran needles through my packages of Dienbienphu cigarettes and presumed to declare my baggage *contraband!* And I said you guys are crazy why'n'cha hit me or something so I'll *really* hate my government, you're proving all my worst paranoias, you really are a pack of hateful murderers and thieves. And all this time Lehrer running around outside Logan Airport saying I'm an MIT professor and I demand his release! and stuff like that. But they finally did let me go (couldn't give me back to Pan Am, after all) and I registered that afternoon, with five minutes to spare, as a Graduate Prize Fellow at Harvard University, to which I would fly from D.C. on Fridays, in order to turn their $250 monthly over to LNS, which now was really and truly a force in the old world.

CHAPTER TWO

The great siege and elevation of the Pentagon

Washington, D.C., is a city of transients. From the highest government officials to the meanest unemployed freeman, everybody there seems to be biding time toward an eventual return "home." Only the black population, which represents 70 percent of the inner city, is stable, and for that reason alone should control the government of the District of Columbia. But, of course, the white careerists, from young Peace Corps personnel to old presidents, have the city in their firm grasp. Until 1964, there was no popular vote in D.C., and at present the people vote only once every four years, and only for the President. Their electoral-college strength, three votes, makes one's vote in Washington worth about one third what it would be worth in Cambridge, Mass., according to Martin Jacobs, a mathematician at Fairleigh Dickinson University. (Parenthetically, one's vote has been shown to be worthless *everywhere,* but the mere fact of its availability is enough to convince many people that they are in control of their destinies. Not so in Washington, where even the "mayor" is White House appointed, and the candidates for the White House, save symbolic candidacies, could not possibly represent the interests of the city's people.) The climate is clammily cold in winter and ferociously hot in summer. There is no publicly operated transportation. The architecture of federal buildings may be beautiful to a certain mind's eye, but to mine it is stodgy, institutional, and repressed. The arts have never thrived in Washington, and the Johnson years didn't help much. The ratio of police per capita is the highest in the land, and the police are wont to arrest and jail

15

people on charges as flimsy as jaywalking. Apartment and house rentals are generally as expensive as in New York City. The best of the federal archives and most significant of congressional sessions are closed to all but journalists and others carefully screened by the authorities and deemed to be, at worst, physically and intellectually harmless. In all, then, Washington is not the ideal city for long-haired, self-conscious subversives to settle into. Time has proved to us that its chief merit is in comparison to *worse* places (e.g., Chicago).

But we chose to begin there for two reasons, one practical and the other ideological. First things first, we were bound to stay there by virtue of having signed leases on our homes and lacking enough funds to manage a move. Secondly we reasoned that D.C. is the center of power in the United States and that, by our very presence, we were bound to learn the intimate workings and faults of the government—keep an eye on the bastards. This naïve assumption died long before our lease expired, and in the meantime the bastards learned to keep a fairly close eye on *us*. We grew quickly accustomed to the presence of the metropolitan police cruiser parked in front of the door of our house all night long every night of the year, and to the FBI agents who periodically called for a session of coffee, tea, and interrogation.

Our house on Church Street was one of those three-story brownstones with a sickly flower garden in front for which Washington is famous. Our block was almost entirely white although bordered by neighborhoods entirely black, an arrangement which astonished nobody and left us conveniently available for night raids by the local burglars. Unlike the neighbors, though, we never bothered to call the police when the TV was discovered stolen, for summoning the gendarmes was sure to add insult to injury. Our house was large enough, at first, to accommodate four or five full-time people at home, and also a functioning office environment. Within two months of our moving in, it became large enough to be a hospital as well, as thousands of our friends and a small percentage of enemies descended on the city to seize the Pentagon.

The weekend of October 21, 1967, was described in the peace movement flyers as a "confrontation with the warmakers," a noble pursuit. The Washington press waxed poetic about its *concern* for the beauty of "our town" and the dignity of the federal monuments these outsiders were certain to defile, if given a chance. The General Services Administration, in charge of city parks and grounds, refused to grant the National Mobilization Committee a parade permit although countless assemblies of Boy Scouts, American Legionnaires, etc. regularly parade the streets with permits routinely requested and granted. As the twenty-first approached, the news broke that ten thousand troops were to be at the ready in nearby Fort Belvoir, Virginia, and God knows how many troops were to be stationed at the Pentagon. Dave Dellinger quit his New York mobilization office to come and haggle with one Harry Van Cleve of GSA over the nonpermit. Robert Lowell, Paul Goodman, Norman Mailer, Benjamin Spock, etc., etc., arrived. The government was preparing for the first time in decades for a serious threat to its Capitol, by its own citizens, over an unpopular war. The World War protesters, the Bonus Marchers, the 1963 civil rights march were not akin to this. This could only be compared to the burning of Washington in 1812. The *Post, Star,* and *Daily News* and all television stations warned the populace, in so many words, to retreat to the privacy and safety of their homes.

Our home was something less than private and always had been. Bloom and I saw the Pentagon weekend as an excellent opportunity for the first meeting of the underground press, and we had for weeks been planning and advertising such a gathering, to be held at the Institute for Policy Studies, the sugar daddy of New Left operations in the area and one of the few left-oriented research institutes in the nation. We saw the meeting as our chance to cement into one movement the independent journals which had sprung up across the country; we wouldn't make that mistake again.

The meeting began in mid-afternoon Friday, October 20, the day before the Pentagon confrontation, in an abandoned loft on Corcoran Street, the IPS building proving too small for our numbers, which were in the hundreds. After Marshall initiated some order with his gavel (a skull on a spring which went Boing! rather than Bang! when pounded on the table) we proceeded to evict such members of the enemy camp as we could identify. First to go was a black reporter (clever!) from the *Washington Post*, then several very police-looking young men with ties. Somehow, *Time* magazine escaped the purge for, in the midst of these formalities began a lengthy monologue by Kenneth Anger, the film-maker whose work usually emphasizes homosexual themes (*Scorpio Rising, Fireworks*). Anger, wearing wraparound dark glasses, was seated atop a tall ladder distributing drugstore sunglasses from a cardboard box on the premise that they protected against the effects of tear gas and chemical MACE, and railing at Shirley Clarke, another film-maker (*The Cool World, Portrait of Jason*) who, Anger claimed, was rich. Shirley maintained she was penniless and kept filming the proceedings in her hand-held camera style, prompting Anger to accuse her of being in the pay of the cops, prompting somebody else to evict Anger, who retreated to the infamous Trio Restaurant on 17th Street.

Being rid of a loud film-maker (whose last remark was to the effect that M. Bloom must be a dirty authoritative Trotskyite), we went on. Marshall began to speak of the goals of Liberation News Service—to provide a link among the antiestablishment presses, to offer hard information to the Movement, etc.—when the staff of the *East Village Other*, led by Walter Bowart in Indian headdress, began a lengthy poem about the underground and an enthusiastic pitch for the fraternal order of the Underground

Press Syndicate, which *EVO* directed. This brought Michael Grossman and Margie Stamberg of the *Washington Free Press* to their feet with charges of embezzlement against the Underground Press Syndicate and *EVO*. John Wilcox, who writes a series of books on visiting various nations on five dollars a day, speaks with a clipped British accent, and publishes a personal paper, *Other Scenes*, quickly corroborated that *EVO* was staffed by a pack of thieves and offered to take over UPS himself if all present were in accord. Before the issue could be resolved, however, Allen Cohen of the *San Francisco Oracle* rose to read a poem, precipitating a lengthy East-West poetry competition between the New York Indian forces of *EVO* and the *San Francisco Oracle* Hari-Krishna heads.

And so it went in that terrible loft. The college editors were interested mostly in campus revolution, the pacifists in the war, the freaks in cultural revolution and cultural purity. The underlying buzz became a steady roar; Marshall burned his draft card, donned his Sgt. Pepper coat, with epaulets and tails, and quit the podium; a few fist fights broke out between warring factions of the antiwar forces; somebody shouted, *in re* the organization of LNS, "Do your thing, do your thing! If we like it, we'll send you money when we can!" I went home to discover an obviously dangerous boy in my bed who, I was warned, was under the influence of some exotic drug which caused him to snarl at me and retreat into the corner. Our glorious scheme of joining together the campus editors, the Communists, the Trots, the hippies, the astrology freaks, the pacifists, the SDS kids, the black militants, the Mexican-American liberation fighters, and all their respective journals, was reduced to ashes. Our conception of LNS as a "democratic organization," owned by those it served, was clearly ridiculous; among those it served were, in fact, men whose very lives were devoted to the principle that no organization, no institution, was desirable. And I have come, through a painful route, to the same conclusion. Seemingly,

the only guaranteed point of agreement between any two
people in that loft was universal opposition to the war in
Vietnam as a crime against humanity; yet many believed
it was impossible to organize a campaign which will end
the war. And it has yet to be done. But the actions of indi-
viduals, each of us, cannot but be significant.

At any rate, it was clear on first meeting our
constituency, that LNS was to be an uneasy coalition.

*   *   *

And what of the great siege and elevation of the
Pentagon? That is history; most of you know what happened there. Between 100,000 and 250,000 persons
marched on the war factory to announce their disapproval
of mass murder in Vietnam; some 660 were arrested, myself included, by federal marshals who did not hesitate to
break the bones and crack the skulls of the most gentle
people, in pursuit of "lawnorder"; although many an
OMMMM Shantih failed to elevate the Pentagon building,
they raised the spirits of a cold and lonely multitude on the
Pentagon lawn, and in foreign lands afar; several of those
jailed are still in jail, or in St. Elizabeth's Hospital for the
mentally disturbed, today, as a result of their experience;
but most of us are still around, and still refusing to cooper-
ate with that war, which is still going on.

*   *   *

LNS published nine stories and a group of photographs about the Pentagon demonstration, including an account by two of the many GIs stationed there to guard the
demonstrators, a narrative by myself about the scene in
Lorton Prison, and documentation of the use of tear gas
against peaceful demonstrators. (The Washington press
had picked up and printed as truth the Army's contention
that the only tear gas used was thrown by the demonstrators *against themselves*. We would have believed this unlikely charge ourselves had we not seen the gas being used,

by the troops, and felt its impact.) Our version of the weekend was printed, in part or whole, in over one hundred newspapers with a total readership in the vicinity of a million. Not bad, we thought, for our third week.

Three Thomas Circle Northwest

"I wasn't talking about knowledge . . . I was talking about the mental life," laughed Dukes. "Real knowledge comes out of the whole corpus of the consciousness; out of your belly and your penis as much as out of your brain and mind. The mind can only analyse and rationalize. Set the mind and the reason to cock it over the rest, and all they can do is criticize, and make a deadness. I say *all* they can do. It is vastly important. My God the world needs criticizing today . . . criticizing to death. Therefore let's live the mental life, and glory in our spite and strip the rotten old show. But mind you, it's like this: while you *live* your life, you are in some way an organic whole with all life. But once you start the mental life you pluck the apple. You've severed the connexion between the apple and the tree: the organic connexion. And if you've got nothing in your life *but* the mental life, then you yourself are a plucked apple."

D. H. Lawrence, *Lady Chatterley's Lover*, 1928

The Pentagon had been elevated, it seems, and everybody went home. Except for our group of new media freaks. We suddenly realized that we *were* home, an island of living guerrilla energy amid the enemy's home camp. It was all so like Saigon, we fantasized, and our job, apart from "revolutionizing the national media," was then to build a Liberated Zone within Washington, a clump of Free Land from which the next, the *real*, Pentagon seizure could be directed. The months ahead were to fill out the metaphor elegantly—I lived to see machine-gun nests set up on the Capitol steps—but we had no way of knowing that the march on the Pentagon was to be the last massive group action for years to come. It was late 1967; Lyndon Johnson was President and would, we presumed, run again; and our movement was one of peace, sanity, and full enjoyment of the senses—we were in pursuit of happiness, LBJ in dictation of misery.

It is impossible for me to describe our "ideology," for we simply didn't have one; we never subscribed to a code of conduct or a clearly conceptualized Ideal Society and the people we chose to live with were not gathered together on the basis of any intellectual commitment to socialism, pacifism, anarchism, or the like. They were people who were homeless, could survive on perhaps five dollars a week in spending money, and could tolerate the others in the house. I guess we all agreed on some basic issues—the war is wrong, the draft is an abomination and a slavery, abortions are sometimes necessary and should be legal, universities are an impossible bore, LSD is Good and Good For You, etc., etc.—and I realize that marijuana, that precious weed, was our universal common denominator. And it was the introduction of formal ideology into the group which eventually destroyed it, or more properly split it into bitterly warring camps—but more on that story later. One reason why legislators could safely ignore irate anti-war letters from their constituents, I am sure, is that the lawmakers themselves, and the enormous majority of ordinary people, can find time to concern themselves only with that which directly affects their personal comforts and securities. Ideology, or the power of ideas, is a feeble power indeed in my country. Thus it is not surprising that the young, who have everything to lose (e.g., their lives) and nothing to gain from the war, not to mention the job-family-corporation cycle and the university's regimen, have carried on the principal burden of the fight.

In short, I am not about to recount the ideas which LNS published or describe the contents of your average underground newspaper—you know all that stuff anyway. It is important for you to understand *the way we lived:* because perhaps in retelling it I too will understand it better ("by-and-by"), for to paraphrase Dylan Thomas, I'm still living it and know it horribly well—and yet much remains to unseal the blind tombs of my mind.

         ✿   ✿   ✿

On December 1, 1967, the Liberated Zone moved its physical reality from our sagging Church Street brownstone to a decrepit three-story office building at Number Three Thomas Circle Northwest, which boasted *two* underground levels. The building was an offshoot of Washington's curious urban development, in which shiny towers and purplish monuments rise alongside structures unfit for human habitation. The Liberated Zone shared Thomas Circle with Lyndon Johnson's own church, the National City Christian, which resembles a Greek temple with its phony acanthus and sleek marble columns; the Hotel Americana, a semicircular mold of glass and steel graced by a heated, domed swimming pool where a poor hip could, with luck, cop a free swim by *seeming* to be *with* some young hotel guest; the all-night People's Drug Store, which locks all but two of its doors at sundown to halt the flow of free merchandise out its portals, and sells plastic hamburgers wrapped in cellophane which you heat up yourself in a special two-minute X-ray machine; a variety of cheap rooming houses; an old red-brick Baptist church, where one may get free food during periods of civil insurrection; a tawdry grocery store where every known Girlie and Boyo magazine is sold; and a colorful assortment of pimps, hustlers, prostitutes, petty thieves, and alcoholics. The State Department and *Washington Post* are around the corner, the White House is six blocks away, the local police precinct nine blocks, and the heart of the Northwest ghetto— SNCC and SCLC country, 14th and U—ten blocks.

By the time we moved there the house on Church Street had become quite full and was no longer sufferable as an office as well—eight phones, each with five blinking buttons, assured irregular and difficult sleeping hours in all the bedrooms; and the bedrooms, as you shall see, were quite noisy enough as it was. Posters lined the walls in indiscriminate ideological conflict—the Beatles alongside Ché Guevara, and Mao Tse-tung with a disrespectful pink bubble pasted on his nose. Stereos copped from middle-class relatives, or purchased (as in my case) during the days when we held straight jobs, rang out with Bob Dylan, Phil Ochs, Ravi Shankar, Monteverdi, Bach, the Rolling Stones, Jimi Hendrix, and Walt Disney's Greatest Hits ("When you wish upon a starrr/Makes no difference who you arrrre"). And these were the people who lived in the rooms and ran the news service and Liberated the Zone:

First there was Marshall Irving Bloom, son of Denver's finest furniture dealer, past editor of the *Amherst Student* at Amherst College in western Massachusetts and founder of the Lecture Series there, and the face that launched the first genuine student uprising in Britain in centuries—London School of Economics, 1966. The issue in London was the appointment of Walter Adams, a white Briton given to strengthening the Empire's firm control over black natives of Rhodesia, as head of LSE. The student protest closed down LSE and killed an elderly porter, who suffered a heart attack at the sight of thousands of students marching on the cathedral. Marshall took upon himself some responsibility for the entirely unforeseeable death of the old man, and today must be hard pressed to discuss the London affair at all—although the Sunday *New York Times* and various British journals occasionally resurrect the incident, usually when a new LSE protest erupts. The *London American*, published for and by U.S. citizens living in or visiting England, published a lead editorial entitled "Bloom, Go Home," and so he did; and at that a full year before Bobbie Dylan's famous advice (in "John Wesley Harding"): "One should never *be* where one does not belong."

Marshall was once described by Steve Lerner in the

Village Voice as "a gaunt young man of insufferable allergies." That he continues to associate with Steve is testament to his boundless respect for the *truth*. He has what seems to some people a nervous and high-strung way of carrying himself, forever fleeing to some other engagement or taking notes or dreaming up apocalyptic schemes or speaking at a pace too rapid to imitate. To some this remarkable performance-in-life seems domineering, unstable, and disconcerting while to those, like me, who love him it is simply his way—unstable no more than any sensitive person would be unstable in our age, and never intimidating. Although Marshall would heatedly and sincerely deny it, everybody else involved would agree that the fortunes of Liberation News Service rose and fell on his shoulders alone; and to his enemies this was anathema while to us his friends it was a natural part of our lives, unobjectionable as the sun and stars and a fact we could understand was appropriate and necessary under the circumstances. His enemies insisted a "radical" news service must be managed by socialists who lived communally and conducted their endeavors as a group, a democratic Team. His friends liked what he did, knew it was good, and encouraged him to do more of it, knowing that *nobody else* could. And this extended argument over Marshall and how we felt about him at last came to be classified, by some, as a difference between "socialists" and "anarchists." An "ideological split" is born. It shall never be said that Marshall left anyone indifferent or unmoved.

He ped-xed all day and hallucinated all night: making the right phone calls, getting bills paid, finding someone to loan a mimeo machine, warding off the collection agencies as a ped-xer (*to ped-x: to manage, work out, solve unpleasant and tiresome duties, such as raising money to live or walking to the store while stoned; cf. San Francisco street-crossing signs, imbedded in the gravel: PED-XING*); and bringing home candy, playing Moroccan music, taking you for a ride in his ridiculous tiny car, understanding your hangups and cheering you up as a hallucinator (*to hallucinate: to have fun, feel free, be easy, be in tune with life, enjoy and understand; opposite of PED-X*). In short he is one of a small group of people alive in the world who can make something out of nothing, nurse an enterprise into a functioning if erratic organization, widely influential if fabulously in debt. Experience has taught me that such rare men often lose control over what they have created from a vacuum. If these were the days of Andrew Carnegie and youth aspired to industrial empire building, Marshall would be very rich—perhaps a furniture tycoon in Denver. As it is, he is quite poverty-stricken, but aren't we all? And he is too kindly and intelligent to be also worldly. In fact, very few of the people in this story are Of This World.

Marshall lived in the big room at the top of the staircase, a good lookout onto the troubled street below; he kept his room scattered with papers and journals atop a colorful Moroccan rug, on which he worked. He was then and is now too hyperthyroid to sit at a desk—and so Letters to the Editor of the *Post*, manifestos for the New Left, and everything else got written on the floor. He sometimes shared the room with Bala-Bala, whose "real" name is forever committed to silence since she is now in hiding from the forces of law, order, and orthodoxy in my country.

Bala-Bala was a secretary, a working girl, when she joined up with Bloom and me in Minneapolis. She lived in a clean, but barely furnished apartment, the address of which she kept secret from her employers and everyone else save Marshall and me. She'd been the kept woman at various times of the son of a former President of the United States, and had roomed with a black lady who later married one of America's most public black militants; she'd been a cocktail waitress, student, and inmate of a "mental hospital"; she'd lived in the mountains with Mexicans and in the cities with rankled business executives; lived high and low, but always *lived*, the apple and the tree all together. She was twenty-two. She lived with us for some months in Washington and later in San Francisco. She is one of the realest, truest persons I have ever fallen in love with. She is tall and blond and incognito, and she might be the ordinary girl sitting next to you on the drugstore lunch-counter stool. If so, if you see her, ask her if she remembers me at all, will you? And tell her, for me, that there is a great peace which lies beyond the war.

Bala-Bala's measure of greatness was that, like Marshall, she was an accomplished ped-xer with sense enough to hallucinate. Although she was decidedly a child of LSD (but aren't we all?), she can get confirmed reservations for The New Media Project on United's flight 308 to Chicago quicker than the Pentagon; and while your average acid-eating freak will be getting arrested for attempting to sit in the park under General Thomas' horse in Thomas Circle (for it is illegal to visit that park, which is picturesquely set in the middle of traffic without cross-walks), Bala-Bala will be tripping off into the night stars, having casually bounced a check off United's friendly hostess.

Next came Little Stevie Wonder, who was sixteen years old and prematurely experienced in the wonderful world of dope, women, and the underground press. He met Harvey Wasserman, a jolly two-hundred-pound Woodrow Wilson fellow (history) at the University of Chicago and former editor of the *Michigan Daily*, on the steps of the Pentagon—and Harvey, who bears uncanny resemblance to Sluggo in the "Nancy" cartoons, gave him a piece of carpet to sleep on in our house. By the time everyone had been bailed out of jail, Stevie had produced a series of magic photographs of the Pentagon event, one of which became a cover for the *San Francisco Oracle* and another an example of "antiwar activity" in the *Atlantic*, and he petitioned us to become LNS photographer in residence. He was gangly and tall and had a crop of curly black hair, not yet long, owing to high-school regulations. He was tired of suburban New Jersey, his parents, his school, and his childhood, and he presented himself to us as a peer while reserving for himself the privilege of halcyon indifference to the needs of the news service since he was, after all, "only a growing boy." I was so old-age as to insist on a letter of consent from his father, and astonished when it arrived promptly in the mail; for we'd housed runaways before and always lived to regret it ("You seem like a nice, educated boy," I recall one harried mother saying as she yanked her daughter from our living room. "Why are you destroying your life like this?").

Stevie was living proof, in our own home, that in our early twenties we were already over the hill. He didn't know about Hesse, Keats, Kerouac, Marcuse, Norman O. Brown, Marx, Leary, or Alan Watts as we did but he lived a bit of all of them. Being two years too young for the draft, he had decided not to bother to register. Being too young to drink, he smoked pot, dropped acid, and at last sniffed heroin (but that's another story); and being too minor to sign contracts, he never worried about the rent, time payments on the press, or the nasty booger from Pitney-Bowes Inc. who periodically called to repossess the postage meter. He hadn't read Zinn, Lacouture, Fall, Robert Scheer, Tom Hayden, or Staughton Lynd but he decided that the war in Vietnam was "bullshit" and he would have no part of it. He characterized Lyndon Johnson not as a war criminal, liar, thief, or any such common terms, but as "an asshole." He had dozens of Little friends around and there are thousands of kids like Stevie all over the United States. He learned faster than we could teach and soon outdistanced us in the lengths to which he would go to express his revolt against the system. He was wide-eyed and bewildered much of the time, picked up and repeated our political views when the occasion seemed to warrant it, and went fishing in Maryland when he was most needed to grind out photographs for the press run. He had an enormous army-surplus overcoat in the immense pockets of which he would shoplift dinner at the local chain grocery when the larder was absolutely bare.

Stevie lived in the basement on a concrete floor covered with mattresses and bamboo curtains rescued from the dump, with an eighty-pound, twenty-two-year-old speed-freak named Robin, who was sharp and tough and could, though white, make her own way in the jungle backstreets of Northwest, and a heroin addict, black, named Romeo, who slept most of the time. He was the classic No-good Boyo of Thomas's *Under Milkwood* and he taught us that an hour could be forever.

Too, there was Lisbeth Aschenbrenner Meisner— Mrs., not Miss. Liz was perhaps twenty-five, a friend of Marshall's at LSE, and just back from a year in the Soviet Union on a Fulbright scholarship. She had married Mr. Meisner in Poland, and until he arrived in the States via Montreal, she lived in the basement room adjoining Stevie's, and played Bach to his Beatles. She worked as a research assistant to I. F. Stone, who sometimes lunched with us on Wednesdays after dropping off the *Weekly* at the printer's, and who told us to make the news service "independent" of SDS and everybody else if we didn't want to end up the mouthpiece of an established political group. Liz had the credentials, degrees, experience, charm, and beauty to be something better than a secretary and mother to a mangy group of seekers, it seemed to me, but then what were the alternatives? The *Washington Post* pays much better than Izzy Stone (and, at that, LNS usurped much of her salary), but the mere presence of the *Post* on our doorstep was trying enough, and Lisbeth, who took seriously all the acts which America performs abroad *in her name,* could never see herself on the Russian Desk at the *Post* or "at State," for you must understand that those two desks are organically connected. She was physically in love with good food, fine wines, her old man in Poland, but even more fiercely partisan to the *idea* we were entertaining: a news agency to the dispossessed! A spokesman for the new culture! She had long brown hair, was strong and almost overwhelmingly well read and bright, and would lecture me on the importance of keeping the *idea* alive when it seemed most difficult, and being *kind* to myself and the others. If I, at twenty-one, could be Stevie's doddering prudent uncle, Liz, at twenty-five, could be my auntie in this microcosmic New Age family. The only known photograph of Lisbeth has her brandishing a strip of Franklin D. Roosevelt stamps (postage had just gone to six cents, to our enormous chagrin since we spent more on stamps than on spaghetti) across her chest, with a wide grin. "Good old" Liz knew where the stamps were kept as well as how Lenin organized the masses.

About Elliot Blinder I could only say that he was free—and freedom cannot be adequately described; it must be experienced. Whereas we could be angry with Stevie for going fishing when all of the anti-war movement *needed* his photos, it was impossible to ever *expect* tireless devotion and slavish duty from Elliot's serene composure, although much of himself was freely given. He'd been editor of his high-school newspaper in Syosset, New York, and had worked with me as layout editor of the *Boston University News*—a good man on graphics, as they say in the trade. He was an inveterate head, forever floating through life, far more a hallucinator than a ped-xer, a serious disciple of Leary, Alpert, Watts, et al., and member of the Neo-American Church, whose sacraments are peyote and LSD. He managed, nonetheless, to successfully struggle for hours with the various duplicating machines at the Institute for Policy Studies, where we printed the first twenty-five or so issues of the news service under the somewhat reluctant aegis of the IPS staff of academic lefties; but he finally left Washington in reaction to the fact that LNS was "too political" and D.C. too basically inferior to Boston as a home base for tripping and rapping. Elliot was soft-spoken, twenty, and very hairy, and lived in the tiny upstairs room-with-a-porch which overlooked the alley between Church and Q—the room which was later to become Miss Verandah Porche's worldwide headquarters of the Bay State Poets for Peace.

I found the words to describe Elliot, though they are not my own. They were written by William Gass, a philosopher and member of That *New York Review* Crowd, with whom I shared visions of Armageddon one dull morning at Purdue University. From his novel, *Omensetter's Luck*:

> "The way you walked through town . . . carrying your back as easy and as careless as you would a towel, newly come from swimming always, barely dry you always seemed, you were a sign. Remember the first evening when you came? You were a stranger, bare to heaven really, and your soul dwelled in your tongue when you spoke to me, as if I were a friend and not a stranger, as if I were an ear of your own. You had mud beneath your arms, mud sliding down the sides of your boots, thick stormy hair, dirty nails, a button missing. The clouds were glowing, a rich warm rose, and I watched them sail 'til dark when I came home. It seemed to me that you were like those clouds, so natural and beautiful. You knew the secret: how to be."

Also there was Max Smith, who called himself just Smith, and his lover Abigail, a seer and card reader late of Berkeley, and they lived all over the house until Max's aunt died and left him enough of an inheritance to take a room elsewhere and write short stories for the hell of it. Smith was a Missouri hillbilly, thirty years old, who met Marshall at the New Politics Convention in Chicago in September, 1967, and came along for the ride; and who, though he wrote news stories very poorly, always leaving out the source of his information or the number arrested, played a heavy guitar and cheerfully cleaned up our generally filthy home and office. He spoke with his hands, seldom offered any opinion or advice, and nodded omnisciently to express approval. There is one known photo of him as well, holding a wet mop and grinning easily under his moustache.

And finally there was me. I lived in the big room next to Marshall's which looked out onto the everlasting alley and slept with a variety of friends on a big red double mattress on the floor. All I can say for myself is that I tried my best to keep the cockroaches from completely overtaking the house, but ultimately lost the battle. There have been cockroaches everywhere I have lived, from early childhood, except for the little Vermont mountain farm which I now inhabit (which has skunks, porcupines, and deer instead). I am thus relieved to learn at last that it was not me alone which brought the roaches, but something about class; and as I now live in the woods, in a frigid climate, the roaches will never come for it's Too Far to Walk, even considering the goodies I leave around.

*   *   *

The sudden acquisition of an office building in a "respectable" (read "white") part of town raised the new problem of collaboration, since LNS alone could neither meet the monthly rent (three hundred dollars) nor fill all of the floors with people and equipment. Our people have been briefly introduced to you, although hosts of others were also involved and some of them will enter the picture a little later; our equipment consisted of one 1932 IBM electric typewriter ("The Crapola") purchased for eighty dollars from Sam the junkman up on 18th Street. Since nobody got a "salary," master's degrees or not, our only expenses were for postage, paper, and telephones, which together quickly ran to two thousand dollars a month almost from the outset. Needless to say, we stole where we could, calling it "liberation of urgently-needed matériel," and we left many bills unpaid. All of our "news," which cut an astonishingly wide swath across the colleges, anti-war groups, government committees, sundry riots, GI bases, and many foreign countries, came by mail or phone at first —we knew reliable if slightly freaked-out people all over the U.S., and met more every day. Our friends told their friends, and before long we were getting signed, unsolicited articles from as far afield as Peking and as nearby as Baltimore. But the new building called for some serious furniture—groups of like-minded people to rent the empty office space, and some superduper twentieth-century communications equipment. Or so it seemed to us in those giddy hours when we smoked dope in the long, empty corridors.

We had the idea then that it would be exciting and impressive for all the anti-war and hip groups in Washington to share one downtown center. I gather in retrospect that this notion was inspired in part by New York's 5 Beekman Street (now, after twenty years, moved to 339 Lafayette Street), where the War Resisters League provides quarters for a half-dozen related activities. The difference in our case was that LNS did not propose to coordinate or otherwise exercise judgment on the groups in the building, which were to be independent partners in a cooperative venture. It had also not occurred to us, although it well might have, that such centralization of "our people" was bound to make us an easy target for the police, the Congress, even the American Nazis over in Arlington. And we remained to learn that it is difficult to remain "independent" of aggressive young Trotskyites when you share a bathroom with them. The same danger which lay dormant beneath the concept of the news service, the impossibility of reconciling all the ferociously partisan outfits which claim a role in one movement, plagued the establishment of our Liberated Zone.

It seemed we had two alternatives: we could give over two floors to the National Welfare Rights Organization, an interracial lobbying group for welfare recipients, whose staff members were mostly in their thirties and clean-cropped; or we could split the floors into offices for the *Washington Free Press*, the local SDS chapter, the Washington Area Resistance (there was so little of this that Marshall and I once turned in our outdated draft classification notices with them in order to raise their public numbers to four), Washington Area Mobilization to End the War (mostly graying Jewish mamas and papas), Insurgent Graphics and Printing (the name was changed, as the mood turned, to *Yippie* Graphics and Printing), *Gor-*

don Free News (a junior high school underground monthly), Dick Gregory for President Campaign Headquarters, and, later, the Young Socialist Alliance (of the Trotsky persuasion). We chose the latter course for we wanted to give all those fledgling groups a home and the young men of Welfare Rights wore *ties*. How shocking it is, a year or two later, to discover that welfare is suddenly *the issue*, and the young men with ties are arousing people to a passion over their *own* rights which they could never reach over anything as distant and abstract as "socialism" or even "the war."

And so the freaks came, came from all the neighboring blocks and cities three thousand miles away, and the police and the press right on their heels. Posters of Malcolm X and Ho-Ho-Ho-Chi-Minh flyers flapped in the breeze in plain view of Lyndon Johnson's own Sunday refuge. The dirty windows of the old building were thrown open with a lusty yank. The old wooden signs identifying this as the home of Soul Records, Inc., were unscrewed and psychedelic nameplates nailed on the door with all the passion of Martin Luther. "Basement: Insurgent Graphics." "DEMO Thursday! Be there!" "Better Living Through Chemistry." Everyone's unused back issues, mimeo equipment, battered suitcases, began to pile up in the halls until passage became wide enough for only one thin person at a time. (No problem there, there were no fatties in our midst.) Last week's half-eaten Eddie Leonard's Shop tuna sandwiches sent out a powerful beam to the neighborhood rats, who lost no time muscling in. Gary Rader, a handsome blond Green Beret who burned his draft card in uniform, was commissioned to carry black wooden desks up the dark stairwells on his back. A healthy army of beaded, painted stoop-sitters took up sitting on the stoop, while Stevie (always most resourceful in such matters) discovered that the roof could be as sunny and airy as Laguna, and group siestas at noon became the rage up there. The plumbing groaned, coughed, and went into a reluctant renaissance. I discovered the miracle of water-based paint. A local construction site was raided by night and enough sawhorses and planks stolen to make desks. Green filing cabinets with ten-degree tilts to starboard sat mutely on the sidewalk, waiting to go into creaking service, while curious pedestrians walked around them. A lad whose voice had not yet cracked, but who claimed to be sixteen, was living in the second-floor closet; Marshall gave him five dollars to invest in *Free Presses* for street sale, but he spent it on grass. A man from the telephone company arrived— did we want to be listed in the Yellow Pages under "News Service—Radical" for as little as five dollars a month? We didn't. Just to make everything official, we startled the local bank teller with a new checking account, "The Liberated Zone." Four different people could sign it.

Deliveries began to be made. First five hundred, then a thousand pieces of mail a day in three separate bundles. A thousand pounds of blinding magenta paper from that nice Mrs. Shapiro at the paper warehouse, whose son had been drafted to Vietnam. Telegram for "Motha": COME HOME ALL IS FORGIVEN DAD. "I'm sposda deliver this collator to the Liberated Noose, this the place?" My FBI agent, Philip Mostrom, took up a stool at People's: "Just coffee." The precinct paddy wagon parked outside—just in case. Nonetheless the pungent odor of marryjuwanna floated out every open window, proof positive that even the clearest risk of arrest will never stop every mother's son from smoking the stuff that lifts him above the horrors and emptiness of American streets. Ugly. Ugly. Ugly. Got to make a Liberated Zone out of your mind and *in* your mind in order to escape the creeping meatball! That lovely joint stands between you and the White House. The Congressional Record was delivered:

AMERICONG OPEN HEADQUARTERS IN NATION'S CAPITAL

"*In the House*: Mr. YOUNG, Missouri: Ladies and Gentlemen, now the American Cong have blatantly an-

nounced revolutionary headquarters right here in our nation's capital! . . . Mr. and Mrs. America, how long will
we allow this to go on?"

We immediately ordered two thousand orange-on-
black lapel buttons: I AM THE AMERICONG. They too
were delivered. The lights burned all night.

Down in the subbasement was Thomas Loves You
(when directly addressed, "Thomas Loves *Me*"), the ener-
getic fourteen-year-old commander of the *Gordon Free
News*, who played hooky from junior high in order to study
rare Semitic scrolls at the Smithsonian. His office was cold
and dark at all times and very wet in the spring, so planks
were found to make a bouncy floor and a cat was hired to
chase the rats, and shit in the corner, giving the *Gordon
Free News* the appearance and odor of a very far underground sheet. Just above Thomas, in the basement, was his
mentor Dick Ochs, thirty, and his anti-war machine (Insurgent Graphics), which sported a live daffodil in its water
trough and feebly printed posters and leaflets for the community; and Stevie's darkroom which, although it *was*
dark, never acquired enough real equipment to be of much
use. On some occasions, our photos were printed with
Washington Post facilities since we had secret sympathiz-
ers riddled throughout that journalistic hippo. (In fact, although LNS used a considerable amount of talent and
machinery from the *Post*, I am pleased to say we *never lost
a man* to it. We were never even solicited.) The rest of the
basement was given over to used collators and presses
which never performed *properly*, bought and charged by
LNS shortly after we occupied the building.

The first floor was the home of the *Free Press*, a bi-
weekly specializing in lurid colors, wretched typography,
and anguished struggle with the politics of communal living. Since the *Free Press* never had an "editor" or "business
manager," it was presumed that the "entire staff" made
all the decisions. But the newspaper itself gave the impression that nobody made any decisions. Meetings of the
"entire staff" were periodically called (it was always dif-

ficult to determine exactly who could vote and who could not since tripping adolescents arrived yesterday would announce themselves members of the "entire staff" and nobody was authorized to deny it) and at times lasted as long as ten or twelve shouting hours. Ideological splits developed and people I had just become accustomed to seeing around the *Free Press* office were hitchhiking back to Texas. The paper was sold on the streets for twenty-cents-the-copy by whoever was poor enough to do it, and had a following among government employees as well as Georgetown freaks (a PR man for the Office of Economic Opportunity told me that "all the boys at OEO," not to mention at Peace Corps, bought and read the *Free Press* and liked to know "what you kids are thinking"). I am sure an occasional copy ended up in the White House. And I'm embarrassed in retrospect that the chief voice of the anti-war movement in the District of Columbia clouded its message with so much of what Lenny Bruce would call "ordinary tits-and-ass," as distinguished from *intelligent* tits-and-ass (like Paul Krassner's *Realist*). The leading lights of the *Free Press* ranged the full spectrum from Mike Grossman, a pudgy curlyheaded junior Norman Mailer always into fistfights (and who once broke the finger of Roly Koefud, editor of Boston's *Le Chronic*, in some fraternal argument or other) to Art Grosman (no relation) who was as gentle and fluid as Connie's Mellors in *Lady Chatterley's Lover*. Too, there were ex-professional men like Bill Blum, formerly with the State Department, and Allen Young, formerly with the *Post* and the *Christian Science Monitor*. Allen also worked with LNS and now heads the New York City office "opposite Grant's Tomb." Many of the *Free Press* folk lived in a haunted house at 12th and N Sts, a cavernous and utterly unfurnished affair where the vibes were nearly as chaotic as in the office.

The second floor housed Mobilization, known for its excellent electric typewriters, the Young Socialist Alliance, known for its evangelicism, Dick Gregory headquarters, known for its splendid namesake, SDS, and The Resistance—the latter two eventually merging to share the thirty-dollar monthly rent. Resisters kept a commune way out near Columbia Road, and SDS, on Corcoran Street. And the physical presence of SDS raised a new problem of collaboration.

In New Left circles at the time, Students for a Democratic Society was indisputably the largest and most influential organization; it has never been, as J. Edgar Hoover would have you believe, an organized cadre preparing to bring down the republic with howitzers and Molotov cocktails. Indeed, when the republic falls, it will be a case of self-destruction, I am convinced (for what civilized society *deliberately* poisons its air and water, makes fresh food illegal, gears for nuclear holocaust?). But it was impossible to get around SDS as something of a common denominator for young insurgents, and for LNS to criticize SDS, which it did, was exactly parallel to the *Post* criticizing Lyndon Johnson, which it didn't—at least not substantially. The White House, it is often whispered, will cease granting "favors" (such as scraps of information!) to correspondents of newspapers which publish a "negative" view of its affairs; just so would SDS cease to be quite "fraternal" with a radical news service which did not adhere to its line. At the very moment while the SDS national office in Chicago was condemning the Youth International Party's (YIPPIE) plans to piss on the Democratic Party convention, LNS was the chief agent publicizing YIPPIE in the subterranean prints. And the names of Bloom, Mungo, Blinder, et al. appeared alongside Jerry Rubin's on the YIP manifesto now held by Mayor Daley to be proof of, among other things, a sinister conspiracy to assassinate himself! The semiofficial view of SDS was that no national radical news agency could *survive* unless organically linked with a national radical Political Party—i.e., SDS. Carl Davidson wrote it up in *New Left Notes*, stating that SDS needed a better "propaganda machinery" and coyly suggesting that LNS should properly be It. For a few weeks I tried to convince myself that I was being *politically immature* to recoil at the word "propaganda," but I couldn't help myself. (Bourgeois hangup?) LNS rejected the proposed affiliation with Students for a Democratic Society.

Unfortunately, the official policemen of American mores, men like Hoover, Daley, and now Nixon, refuse to draw the fine distinctions between different kinds of dissident citizens which I am here laboring. Daley appears on my TV screen to say it is a conspiracy among three men— "Rubin, Hayden, and Dellinger, Rubin, Hayden, and Dellinger"—which led the assault on his fair burg. Rubin is a brilliant anarchist, Hayden a conscientious socialist, and Dellinger an uncompromising pacifist, but these labels conveniently fit into a single nefarious category in Richard Daley's crippled vision. Thus are we cast afloat in a dangerous sea, together in spite of ourselves yet forever separate by passionate will.

✿   ✿   ✿

Meanwhile up on the third floor, where LNS lived, everything was happening too fast. It soon took us all day just to open the mail and answer the phones, which were everywhere, it seemed. All attempts to divide and categorize the work—Stevie must answer mail requests for Howard Zinn's article "Dow Shalt Not Kill" (we sold twenty thousand), Liz must screen the phone calls and get rid of bill collectors, Allen Young must drive his Volkswagen to the post office—failed miserably in the rush of work undone. Everybody was trying to keep up with insurrection in colleges, ghettos, and hip communities all at the same time. "Max, have you called Orangeburg, South Carolina, yet?" Cleveland? St. Louis? Norman, Oklahoma? Everybody wondered aloud whether any checks had come in the day's mail (subscribers were advised to pay fifteen dollars monthly for the service, although many couldn't afford to and paid less or nothing)—and could we thus go to the movies tonight? The number of underground newspapers went from fifty to a hundred to three hundred in a matter of a few months, and as 1968 came upon us, there were suddenly *straight* newspapers too, dailies in Pennsylvania and Iowa and California, who wanted to print our copy, dying to know where it was *at*. The mass media—UPI, the *New York Times*, CBS News—decided that we were a reliable source of information about the movement, and we had to dance around their questions. Meanwhile, mailings of LNS were getting fat and frequent—three times a week.

We looked for help wherever we could find it. One apparent break came in December when SNCC founded an Aframerican News Service in Atlanta to specialize in news of black power. We instantly effected an exchange relationship with them, grateful for some hard stuff written by blacks, who were in those days justifiably suspect of the white left and its neuroses. ANS began to crowd out LNS in ghetto newspapers like Cleveland's *Plain Truth* and Albany's *Liberator*, but we were delighted. And, toward the end of December, came the remarkable Telex, easily the most sophisticated device ever put into the hands of movement freaks.

Telex is a trade name of the Western Union Company for a private teletype system used by many fat-cat corporations and the United States Senate and relatively bugproof. A half-dozen machines had been introduced in college newspaper offices while we were with the U.S. Student Press Association, and others were envisioned for Boston, New York, San Francisco, and Chicago. All but the latter came true. Best of all, anybody anywhere could cable news to us—collect, of course—by going to any Western Union office and producing our code number. The Telex news was instantaneous, cheaper than telephones, and already typed with carbons. And just at the moment when the infernal clatter was getting tiresome, we hit upon international Telex (this system is owned by the International Telephone and Telegraph Company, which does not charge a monthly rental fee, so that even the most insolvent enterprise can have one and pay only for time used). And that led to Harry Pincus and Danny Schechter, our friends in London, establishing a European News Service from their ramshackle house on Roslyn Hill and translating LNS into foreign languages at their office in Oxford.

A few days before the Lunar New Year, Howard Zinn and Dan Berrigan, professor and priest, had gone to Hanoi to supervise the release of three American pilots. The Telex rang loudly but I ignored it for a while, for unlike the phones, it did not require immediate tending. I returned to find a solidarity message from the Vietnam Peace Committee, doubtless written by some of the Vietnamese I'd met in Bratislava, and this from Zinn and Berrigan:

> "RELEASE OF THREE AIRMEN IMMINENT. NORTH VIETNAMESE OUTRAGED AT CONTINUING BOMBARDMENT BUT RETAIN COMPASSION FOR AIRMEN WHO ARE TRAPPED BY WASHINGTON DECISIONS. HOPE RELEASED AIRMEN NEVER AGAIN BOMB YET AWARE POSSIBILITY THREE RELEASED PILOTS RETURN TO BOMB VIETNAM. WE ARE MOVED BY NORTH VIETNAMESE STATEMENT "EVEN IF THIS HAPPENS WE RETAIN FAITH IN ULTIMATE DECENCY OF AMERICAN PEOPLE."

*   *   *

WINDOW POEM AT THOMAS CIRCLE

Green with age
and frozen in the saddle,
hat in hand,
with a humble nod
for a hundred-gun salute
(long silent)
sits the model major general George
while a pigeon nestles on his head.
She lifts her leg to lay an egg.

There is little to praise here,
Mother of Cities,
the Washington's Needle,
the Santa Maria,
the Presidential Christian Bank and Tomb;
SPQR on police cars,
Gestapo everywhere—with dogs;
there is little to praise.

And if we cannot praise you
we must bury you,
and while we bury you
how shall we sing?
If we do not smite you,
Gorgon of Cities,
your blood-feathered eagles
will carry us off
to make glue and soap
in our sleep.

I am a gentlewoman,
not given to murder, martyrdom,
or apocalyptic dreams.
Yet in well-lit rooms at midday
the images ooze like auto fumes
as they circle the green
where General Thomas,
greathearted mountie,
watches the traffic,
awaiting the moment to strike.

Verandah Porche

✲   ✲   ✲

Marshall Bloom is now the chief Boo-Hoo of the Neo-American Church in western Massachusetts, where he resides at the LNS Farm in Montague and prepares for the birth of *The Journal of the New Age*; Bala-Bala is in hiding halfway to the Orient; Lisbeth Aschenbrenner Meisner is in Berkeley, doing whatever it is people do in that otherworldly town; Elliot Blinder broadcasts acid rock over an FM radio station in Boston; Max Smith was last seen heading for the Ozarks; and I am winter-bound in Vermont and, of course, writing this story.

And Little Stevie Wonder died of fast cars and exotic pills, mixed, on a New Hampshire quarry road. "He went straight," Marshall said, "while the road turned." Nogood Boyo is on the ultimate trip.

CHAPTER FOUR

The Washington Free Community

Well, I was talking about winter in Washington—
the numb winter of 1967 and 1968—when spring of 1969
arrived in Vermont. That was a couple of months ago, and
you can just *imagine* how happy we were to see the cro-
cuses back. The warmer weather is sure to produce the
biggest population boom in these parts since the hoboes
came to roost, but I figger there'll be just enough to go
around and no more. I was too happy to write this book for
a while there, but here I'm back to resume the story. (It
gets better.) O, the trials of professional freaks; if the wood
supply doesn't run out or the winter winds knock you
down, then brown rice and bad vibes surely will bury your
spirit, but I'm not complaining, I know I'm living the life of
Riley compared to you forty-hour-a-week people out there.
And naturally our effort to do Another Thing apart from
the blessed orders must have its hardships. We get by with
a little help from our friends, half a break on the weather,
and an occasional Burn Scheme or two to relieve utter
bankruptcy. We're unprepared, of course, for the imminent
economic collapse in my country, but there *is* the rhubarb
patch when all else but ecology fails.

Back to Washington. As if to remind myself that it's
still there, I returned in January of 1969, coincident with
Richard Nixon's inauguration. (I had hoped to see *him* as I
don't believe he exists, but caught nary a glimpse as my
view was blocked by about a thousand policemen and one
sixteen-year-old shouting "Up the ass of the ruling class!")
I relearned that the winter in Washington is cold and
windy, yet with little or no snow to cover the city's dull

47

grayness; in short, that it has no more integrity than the government. Walking the streets of Washington, one always stares at the pavement, and is bitterly disappointed when even February's ornery winds won't dump white on that gravel. Hence there was no great rebirth in spring either, just the promise of an uncomfortably *warm* grayness. We lived indoors, behind our paltry barricades, and ignored the streets whenever we were allowed—hardly a People's Park in town worth defending, and the Cherry Blossom Festival was canceled due to riots. Except for an occasional excursion to the Biograph Theatre in Georgetown, one of your supergroovy artsy-fartsy cinemas showing a steady diet of Mae West & Humphrey Bogart (you know the scene), I spent the entire winter in the house, at the office, and within the special world of Eddie Leonard's Sandwich Shops, one of which was conveniently located nearby both. All of Eddie Leonard's shops feature baroque oil paintings of his various sandwiches (Bar-B-Q, Tuna Salad, Eddie's Special) and a midnight clientele just raunchy enough to convince you it's *dangerous* to be in there and yet never really hurt you. I remember Frank Speltz of the *Free Press* telling me, with sparkling eyes, that one advantage of the Thomas Circle location was its all-night Eddie Leonard's, and I forlornly tasting yesterday's Tuna Salad. There never was, for me, a Telegraph Avenue or Harvard Square or Latin Quarter where "our" people regularly congregated although "we" were not an impossibly small constituency in the city. So when the word drifted in that a Washington Free Community was being "organized" for the benefit of all, my first reaction was one of exhilaration.

Cut to the Ambassador Theater on 18th. The Ambassador once housed vaudeville acts, Stepin Fetchit and all that stuff, then second-run movies, and now (it's come to *this*) is used primarily for light shows and local rock groups, secondarily for political rallies, such as the Pentagon Eve spectacle starring Mailer, Goodman, Lowell, &c. (Actually *right now* it's all boarded up and forgotten, but we're talking 1967.) Its typical customer is seventeen years old, female, and lives in Maryland or Virginia. It has neither seats nor carpets, apparently to encourage dancing, although rock being what it is everybody just stands around and grooves on the ear-splitting vibes. It is a mild night for December, just before Christmas, and an Off Night for the Ambassador, which is hosting the first meeting of the Washington Free Community, and all of Our People are there. Most of these people live in communes not unlike Church Street. They include the political freaks from Thomas Circle; the rock entrepreneurs from the theater; the Guerrilla Theater professionals of the American Playground, always planning demonstrations which didn't quite come off; the liberal Christians from the church-coffeehouse Mustard Seed; adolescent habitués of Yonder's Wall in Georgetown, where thirty-eight kids got busted for a single joint; a twenty-five-year-old doctor, Steve Brown, who eventually founded a free medical clinic which is valuable beyond measure and still open; some self-conscious film-makers; and more. Here's the problem, though: most of Our People really don't *like* each other, nor do they have anything in common (except perhaps their political views, which count for very little in *real* life).

The meeting never quite got off the ground (meetings seldom do). Everybody suspected the others of being either impossibly straight or insufficiently militant, I suppose, and the "leaders," those who had called the meeting, accused the lot of us of apathy. "We've just *got* to get our shit together," the theme ran, but the issue of "how?" was never resolved and the more important question "why?" was never asked. Frustration set in (it always does) and, as usual, several people attempted to talk at the same time, precipitating the 934th parliamentary hassle I've suffered since leaving home for college. And finally, it was decided that another meeting would be held. Thereafter, a small group of us drove out to General Lewis Hershey's home in Maryland to serenade him with spiked Christmas carols, and predictably the house was dark and unmoved. I have

thus learned the hard way to assume that nothing will be
accomplished by taking one's case to the men in power for
whether they be university deans, bank presidents, or politicians, they are invariably Out of Town when you need
them. You may be sure that the American male who has acquired wealth and/or power over other people's lives will
be Out of Town most all the time, and you must make him
come to you, notice you, if you expect to get results. I cannot be accused of ever having written *my* Congressman (!)
to protest the war, although my Congressman (at the time,
U.S. Senator Leverett Saltonstall) once wrote a series of
letters to Boston University President Harold C. Case suggesting I be expelled and "thanking God every night that
students like this are in a tiny minority" (ho ho).

    The Washington Free Community held many more
meetings, but I gather attendance lagged, for the leaders
were always complaining about the lack of "community
spirit" among Our People; which reminded me of football
types in high school bitching about "lack of school spirit" if
the stadium wasn't full on an October Saturday. And, just
as in high school, the great majority of people showed excellent judgment in being somewhere else when the group
sessions were going on. My high school was nothing more
or less than a prison of the body and mind, where the students masturbated in the toilet stalls and then were made
to feel guilty about it by Roman Catholic careermen
(themselves *sworn to chastity*); and the Washington Free
Community was bound and restricted from the start by its
dead-wrong assumption that human beings seeking freedom can *act* as a group through a democratic meet-and-
vote process, in short through the *same* system which the
United States uses for placement of its rulers. The American
people may yet vote themselves dead and buried. I have
never voted in my country; but don't let that stop you if it
makes *you* feel better.

    But I'm getting distracted. The whole point is that
a free community does not have meetings, and your attend-

ance is never required in a free community. You are welcome to do whatever comes to mind, so long as it does not actively harm others, in a free community. Nothing is expected of you, nothing is delivered. Everything springs of natural and uncoerced energy. Compassion and understanding will go a long way toward making your community free, delegation of labor will only mechanize it. I have known and even lived in some free communities, but the Washington Free Community was not one of them. Rather, it was plagued by the same fear, suspicion, and distrust which is characteristic of almost all groups on the left in America, and which send them down, time after time, in a fury of civil wars. Those who make a life of seeking power, whether they are members of SDS or the Defense Department, must first establish enemies from whom they will wrest control—and then do it, By Any Means Necessary.

All this is not to suggest that every member of the WFC was greedy and power struck. Most were honorable and decent, many were deeply committed humanists, but all of them together simply could not work as a Unity, or Comm-unity, however noble the original conception. Corporate entities such as the *New York Times,* which *seem* to hold together for many years, do so only under the shadow of some tyrant or other; you have a boss, who has a boss, who has a boss, etc., and he who violates the will of the Maker finds himself quickly purged ("fired"). Since the Makers of the WFC had no such economic power over their constituency, they soon lost it and if the organization has re-formed itself since I left D.C., I do not know of it. (Parenthetically, and finally, I should add that monolithic tyranny directed *against* any class of people from a clearly distinguishable common enemy *will* bring them together, perhaps even make them a free community; viz., the immediate but usually short-lived mass response from college students once their deans have called in the bashers to tear-gas the campus, or the instinctive reaction of black

people to the presence of combat troops in their neighborhoods.)

*   *   *

Alas, the Blue Meanies and politicians in the area
did not see Our People as separate and distinct human
beings at all, and while they never launched a pogrom
thorough enough to make Us fight back together, they nevertheless classed Us as criminals. I remember a certain sergeant telling me, as we strolled to the paddy wagon, that
"you Niggers and longhairs are all the same, bunch of
fuckin' troublemakers." And how I longed for the Niggers
to adopt the same attitude!

The cops seemed to get the notion that the "hippie
problem" in Washington was becoming serious shortly
after the WFC began its meetings, and I can only assume a
causal relationship existed. Led by their fearless com-
mando, Sgt. David Paul, they swept down on Yonder's
Wall in Georgetown one cold night and arrested thirty-
eight persons, most of them minors, for group possession of
one marijuana cigarette. The Wall was a teeny scene, its
proprietor barely seventeen, and not nearly so rotten-to-
the-core as Thomas Circle, but it was public, hence easy
game. The defense attorney for the thirty-eight kids, John
Karr, eventually got the charges dismissed with the argument that since this cigarette was hand rolled, the Wall
could not have been a distribution center for marijuana; if
it *were*, you see, the cigarettes there would be rolled by
machine! The judge found that reasonable and, being unable to single out one of the thirty-eight as the true owner of
the joint, was forced to free the whole group. Another
boner for Dave Paul, and the *Free Press* lost no time in
making it public. Ironically, LNS did not even know of the
Yonder's Wall bust until several days after it occurred, although we'd pick up the number arrested in Berkeley or
Denver moments after it happened, on Telex or from the
phone. So who knows what's happened on *your* block tonight?

❖ ❖ ❖

I interrupt the winter to bring you the summer. I'm in Cambridge, Mass., and it is 5:00 A.M. on a June Sunday. I drove Frieda the VW to Harvard Square from my brother Aanu's place on Dodge Street, thinking to pick up a Sunday *Chicago Tribune,* "The World's Greatest Newspaper," an utterly reactionary and untrustworthy sheet, but very entertaining. Alas, though, I could get only a *Boston Globe* full of liberal claptrap about how *awful* it must be to live in the ghetto and, implicitly, how we must help those people achieve suburbia, and about police and hippies setting up "mutual ground rules" to avoid "trouble" on the "Common." Newspapers which pose as liberal and understanding are the most unbearable, for in striving to, say, "close the generation gap," they embarrass both sides of it. They have so little faith in their own systems and generations that they grow sideburns and praise Eugene McCarthy, hoping that'll be *enough* and of course it isn't and the social friction gets hotter every year. Worst of all are editors and politicians assuming a youthful image without the illogical, spontaneous passions of youth. If I were sixty-five, or even forty-two, I hope I'd be saying: "You kids are welcome to all this bizarre fancy, and I only hope you really enjoy it."

5:00 A.M., Sunday, is the best time to be in Cambridge.

❖ ❖ ❖

When it became a few days before Christmas, somebody said, "Hey, it's a few days before *Christmas!*" and everybody else laughed. The underground papers, which numbered two hundred fifty by that time, had printed almost nothing relating to the most sacred holiday in Western civilization, unless it was sarcastic (e.g., *The Free Press* cover picturing the Virgin, white, swaddling Stokely Carmichael, BLACK, in her arms) or, in a few cases, polemical. LNS published "The Twelve Days of

Vietnam" by Ronald J Willis, founder of a Fortean* institute of underground science in Arlington, Virginia, the chorus of which was "Kill Those Yellow Bel-lies." Nonetheless, all of the college papers and most of the underground ones had suspended publication until the new year, so we decided to take two weeks off. I hadn't been up to New England since the summer, except for an electric *Avatar* benefit with the San Francisco Mime Troupe at B.U., so I decided to go home for Christmas. But my funds collapsed in New York City and I ended the year in a big bed on Prince Street more or less enjoying a weird ménage à quatre with two girls from Boston and a teenage boy from the lower East Side. I can't remember most of what went on there, but I do recall borrowing the exact sum needed for one-way fare on the Congressional Express, and riding back to D.C. with a trainload of drunken sailors and GIs.

The new year, 1968, promised to be one of High Adventure, thrills and spills, a year of enormous success and bitter defeat, a year in which we'd climb the mountain and fall off again. Everybody was excited with the prospects for an explosive year, but few realized just how heavy it would get; I think it would be fair to say that many of Our Kind thought the Republic would fall in 1968. And maybe it did.

Marshall and I flew to Cleveland on New Year's Day for a one-week conference sponsored by the University Christian Movement, which had freely offered to pay our expenses there. All I knew of the UCM was that it was a "liberal" coalition of kids who still went to both church (Protestant, mostly) *and* college, yet sought to be relevant, anti-war, and generally with it. Its director, Leon Howell, was in his early thirties, chubby, and laughed a lot; he was in touch with elements (black youth in South Africa, for example) very important to us and yet somehow missing from the cast of movement characters, out of our reach,

---

* Charles Hay Fort was a scholar of unreported natural phenomena, such as UFO's and psychic confrontations, around the turn of the current century.

and was also one of the most intelligent and humane people working out of New York. I first met him through Jack Smith, an Episcopal chaplain at B.U. and one of our staunchest allies, a peer actually, in what we believed to be our freedom struggle there. (I *still* believe it was a freedom struggle, by the way, but it now seems to have died, or gone astray, or both.) All of which is to say that Christians aren't *necessarily* constipated in this day and age, although they invariably have two strikes against them. The Cleveland conference boasted some excellent hashish, a large Resistance "service" (which combined Christ and Carl Oglesby, an odd but pleasing pair), and the birth of the Student Communications Network (SCN).

The SCN kids—Howard Perdue, Ken Oleari, Orlando Ortiz, Colin Connery—were to form the LNS bureaus in both California and New York, although Marshall and I didn't know that when we met them. In fact, our first impression was negative, for after all, these goyish Youth were *competition* in a field so limited that its establishment ate at Eddie Leonard's. They had already opened a Berkeley office with Telex, and they viewed themselves as a radical alternative to the United States Student Press Association; too, they were at first as jealous of their independence as we were. For six days and nights Bloom & I engaged them in mortal psychic struggle although we were hopelessly outnumbered, about fifteen to two, but on the seventh day we rested. The entire SCN contingent came to our room (in the Sheraton, natch) for a big conference before we went East and they West, and, well, the peace pipe was passed around and soon one and all were as stoned as they ever had been. The lights were dimmed and the giggling was subsiding and of course all talk of the news service had long been abandoned when somebody started to hum, just hum, a long low note. Somebody else counterpointed with a higher note, a hum which sounded curiously like "OM." A third person began a round of notes. Until all of us were singing at the top of our lungs, not a word but an infinitely complex series of pure chants

which formed the most beautiful chorus I have ever heard.
The choir went on for perhaps an hour, reaching a climax
somewhere in the land of the Divine as the powerful dope
worked its magic on our minds. I had not been There before, and I have not been able to return. We fell asleep
shortly after the music stopped and the next day, a Sunday,
determined in a few smiles that the Berkeley SCN office
should also be known as Liberation News Service. Later
that year, Marshall, Verandah, and I were to spend some
weeks with Howard, Ken, and Orlando in Berkeley and
thoroughly enjoy each other's company; to discover that
the Berkeley office was as benignly disorganized as our
own (God has truly smiled on my *karass*); to introduce
Howard and his super keen lady Jane (hiya Jane!
Strawberries-and-cream-for-breakfast Jane!) to Mr. LSD
on Muir Beach, where I was Franklin Roosevelt and Verandah, my Eleanor, à la Ralph Bellamy and Greer Garson
in the movie *Sunrise at Campobello* ("O, Eleanor, who
would think that a mere paraplegic like me will some day
be dictator of the whole world?").

> *Franklin Roosevelt told the people how he felt*
> *And they damn well believed what he said.*
> *He said 'I hate war, and so does Eleanor,*
> *But we can't be safe till everybody's dead.'*

And that's how the New Year began.

Dear reader, now I will tell you about Verandah,
for at about the same moment we were announcing the establishment of LNS West Coast, we were introducing her
as our Poetry Editor. (If you suspect this reference to chronology to be merely a device for changing the subject,
you're one step ahead of me, and congratulations.) Miss
Porche had just come from a doomed relationship with a
certain monk & mystic in Boston, brought only the clothes
on her back and of course the prestige and following of the
Bay State Poets, and moved right into the room-with-a-
porch which Elliot Blinder had recently floated out of. The

first to get hit was little Stevie Wonder, who set to work luring her into his All Grown Up boudoir, but none of us was unaffected by her arrival. Everything in the movement, in the underground press, in fact in the whole city of Washington, D.C., changed for the better when she came. Phil Ochs made a song about it: "She's a Rudolph Valentino fan/And she doesn't claim to understand/She makes brownies for the boys in the band."

Verandah is, simply, the Queen of Poesie. With her have I been in sweet meadow and foul city so I should know. Her eyes are brighter than ever evening star shone over Vermont and her soul darker than ever night sky surrounded it. She knows me and I her, enough at least to love and forbear each other forever. We are splendid chums.

Everybody should read her poems for these are her droppings to polite society. I sure hope everybody doesn't get all hot to meet her too for then she would be forever flying off to Paris or something and no time for fun. She has no grasp of reality, only of the truth. When I have the courage, which is far from always, I read her poems and suffer and smile with them. We have our ups and downs, V and I.

I remembered my first experience with Mr. LSD had been at Verandy's infamous house in Somerville, Mass. ("The Hovel"), where she lived at various times with Richard Schweid, Miss Katz, and Sloth the Cat. Visitors included the likes of Allen Ginsberg and The Chambers Brothers. It was, from about 1965 to 1968, the contemporary parallel to certain nineteenth-century French *salons* but I guess we could play *La Bohème* for only so long. On this first trip, at any rate, we passed Mr. E. E. Cummings' yard in Cambridge and lay laughing hysterically on the grass in front of the Harvard Zoological Museum. We were six years old and I was in college.

"Raymond, what school do you go to?"
"I go to Saint Pat's, where do you go?"
"I go to Lindberg School."
"You a *Protestant* or something?"

"I'm different."

"You ain't a Catlic."

"No, I'm different. (*Pause*) I'm Jewish."

"(*Shocked*) Christ-killer!"

"(*Readily*) We did it and we're glad!"

Academic types smiled benignly on our giddy scene on the lawn. "Here we are on *acid*," I thought to myself, "and *they* think we're just *in love!*"

With Verandah around, it was easier to ped-x all the shitwork which came with printing, collating, and distributing our own product. She took up her throne in the pasting-on-address-labels room, in the kitchen, in the pressroom. She helped alleviate the endless routine of chores which either did not get done (stacks of unanswered mail, unprinted posters, phone calls unreturned) or got half done. And she made a perfect foil for our second new arrival, Allen Young, who came to LNS in December upon resigning from the *Washington Post*, and who now manages the New York office (more about this later). Allen was as workaday as Porche was glamorous, as nervous about the organization's politics and finances as she was out of touch with such affairs, as devoted to the socialist state as she was to The Truth.

So it went in January. There was always too much work to do and we worked all the time with a growing seriousness as the presidential elections approached, the Black Panthers emerged in California, Eugene McCarthy began cutting into our constituency (LNS disavowed his candidacy from the start), and the building next to ours on M Street and Thomas Circle donned a "Students for Kennedy" sign. Our operating premise was that Lyndon Johnson would run again, and he was decidedly our Enemy, however unsure we were of our Friends. Meanwhile, down in New York, something was brewing in Jerry Rubin's apartment which would soon have us in its grasp as well.

Rubin is a thirty-year-old self-conscious theoretician of the movement, anxious to be at the forefront of What's Happening, whether that means the Pentagon confrontation (of which he was "co-director"), the acid-youth culture, or the Democratic convention in Chicago. He might be called a politician, and his special constituency was wont to gather around him in that East 3rd Street dive called home. I've always found his writing very exciting, since he always knew the minds of the most sophisticated movement professionals. But his actual power and constituency was and is very small, and when he personally announced that 500,000 Yippies would demonstrate in Chicago, only the federal government believed him. In fact, Yippie (or Youth International Party) was a conspiracy only in that it didn't *exist* except in the minds of Jerry, Abbie Hoffman, Paul Krassner, Stu Albert, and a few others in New York City, and in the pages of LNS. Those few elements, apparently, were enough to create enormous apprehension in the hearts of the Chicago power structure, the Democratic Party, and millions of Middle Americans, and to send Richard Nixon safely home on 42 percent of the vote.

I guess it only stands to reason that if the *New York Times* is supposedly a Democratic, Jewish paper, then LNS should be Yippie and Neo-American Church. At any rate, when Jerry called from New York with news of Yippie, it was like getting called in by the President. "Why'n'cha come up here an' we'll talk about it?" he said, and so I did, and had a good time at it. And I agreed with Jerry then that it would be a fine thing to encourage everybody (i.e., mostly everybody under thirty) to come to Chicago in August. And by the time I changed my mind, decided I'd rather see live kids than dead revolutionaries come September, it was too late, and the Festival of Life went on without me—and without most of the rock groups, underground newspapers, and hip celebrities we had promised. To this day I have not been able to decide whether it was a Good or a Bad Thing, that scene in Chicago which we effectively caused to happen. On the one hand, many of the people who got stomped, busted, even maimed there knew what they were getting into and did it in the name of revolution ("Some people will do worse things than any cop, and do them in the name of revolution," Eldridge Cleaver once told me), and on the other some of them were fifteen years old, from Long Island, and went there looking for *fun*. Their street drama *did* shock many television viewers into sympathy but it caused many more, inexplicably, to applaud the savagery of the Chicago police. I'd made preliminary trips to Chicago in March and May of 1968, to discover that it was one place, perhaps the only one, where the liberal state would *not* tolerate mass demonstrations without a bloodbath. But the wheels of publicity and national anxiety toward Chicago were grinding at an irresistible pace by January. The Battle of Chicago, given LNS and Yippie and the straight peace movement, was an inevitability.

Our endorsement of YIPPIE also constituted our first serious disagreement with Students for a Democratic Society, which opposed the demonstrations from the first, not especially on the basis of protecting Our People's bodies (although that reason was cited), but because SDS considered the tactic unwise and likely to create more reaction than revolution. Nonetheless, August found many SDS members among the street people. And Jerry Rubin's plans for mass freaking-out (pissing on the cops, kidnapping convention delegates, etc.) were also strenuously opposed by straighter elements in the movement, including the New York pacifist lobby. So, even the most casual observer (and certainly the FBI, which viewed the whole thing with intense interest) could see that the "conspiracy" forming against Chicago was the most public, internally disorganized conspiracy in history. Yet the government, aided by its mouthpieces (the great newspapers in every city) has successfully convinced millions that a real, and dire, underground conspiracy existed and continues to exist. Haw, haw. Off to jail with Jerry Rubin, who was more enthusiastic than prudent.

The underground papers were not universally enthused about Yippie, though; it seems, in retrospect, that the most thoughtful of them (*Avatar*, the *San Francisco Express-Times*, for example) were agin it wholeheartedly, and the least thoughtful, most pornographic ones (*East Village Other*, *Berkeley Barb*, for example) much in favor, with the many papers which lacked real identity just going along with the game, printing word of Yippie plans, etc. LNS caught this split mood before long, and ultimately printed a sizable lot of anti-YIP stuff, but perhaps it was too little too late.

When Lyndon Johnson withdrew from the presidential "race" in March the Yippies were severely hurt, for, as Jerry had written, "No kid in America wants to grow up to be like Lyndon Johnson"; but when Robert Kennedy was shot the following June, they bounced back to life. In the interim, of course, the Washington Free Community fluctuated wildly between hope and despair, ups and downs, and there were even some among us who looked, however reluctantly, to Kennedy for a way out. But back in January, it was all the way with LBJ, and in our contempt for him we never realized our good fortune in having such a clearly contemptible enemy. Occasional opportunities to embarrass his family and dog him with ridicule and guilt were never passed up.

Take the opening night of John Wilson's play *No Man's Land* at the Washington Theater Club, for example. Verandah and I, reading somewhere that this was an anti-war play and being naturally interested from a professional point of view, spent our last few dollars on tickets and went to our seats. There we discovered, to our astonishment, that Lynda Bird and her new hubby, Chuck Robb, were sitting several rows away, directly facing us in the round theater, literally within spitting distance if you can pardon the phrase. And we wasted no time in staring them down, pointing at them with our fingers as the play told of war and execution and evil, even approaching them in the lobby with the whispered admonition, "Executioner." Well let me tell you Lynda Bird was pretty freaked-out by the whole experience—legitimate theater is usually such a comfortably middle-class pleasure—and so were the secret service goons who surrounded us with thinly disguised pistols and Youngstown, Ohio, crew cuts. Verandah was denied entrance to the ladies' room after Lynda went in there. And Lynda B buried her face in Chuck's chest while he grinned a blind, cretinal grin in the face of a great play about murder. The rest of the audience was on the edge of its seat, fascinated by the counterposition of two such worldly lovers and two such raggedy ones, and half expecting shots to ring out, I'm sure. In all, the whole evening was pure psychodrama for both the Robbs and us, and I doubt they returned to that theater (I know we didn't).

Or take the Sunday morning that a pack of us invaded Lyndon's church—which, as I have no doubt already said, was across the street from our office building. The church was the National City Christian, and the way things were going in January of 1968, it was one of the last places left where LBJ could "worship" without fear of being reprimanded from the pulpit. For its minister, Reverend Mr. George Davis, was a friend of the Johnson family and incapable of criticizing it since this friendship was his chief, perhaps only, claim to fame. He was not a hawk or fascist or conscious Pentagon-head exactly, just a poor dumb Christian minister who was always making cloddy-sounding defenses for everything Lyndon did, whether bombing North Vietnam or farting in public. And when Eartha Kitt embarrassed Lady Bird with a few choice words at lunch that January, Reverend Mr. Davis couldn't resist putting his two cents in. And the freaks across the street, reading his two cents in the afternoon papers, couldn't resist stuffing them down his throat the next Sunday.

You, dear reader, will recall that Miss Kitt was (unwisely) invited to lunch by Lady Bird, some kind of women's luncheon for highway beautification affair. And Eartha, who is black and also known as Cat Lady, told Lady Bird where the war in Vietnam *and* marijuana smoking were At among the nation's youth, which left Mrs.

Johnson biting her quavering lip and Mrs. Richard Hughes, wife of the New Jersey governor, protesting that she had seven children and none of *them* would smoke marijuana. (Haw, haw, what she doesn't know won't hurt her.) The underground press soon featured a cartoon of a chuckling LBJ consoling his sobbing wife, "Now, honey, what'd y'all *expect*, invitin' a nigger to lunch?" Reverend Davis, seeking to console the unfortunate First Lady, wired her from a Midwestern city a sharp condemnation of those "ill-mannered, stupid and arrogant persons, including Negroes," who insult the protocol of D.C.'s white civilization.

The following Sunday, nine of us from LNS, the *Free Press*, and assorted Free Community endeavors, plus our faithful lawyer friend Bill Higgs, gathered in the basement in churchgoing clothes which showed signs of being hung in closets or crammed in guitar cases for months or years. I wore my spiffy blue suit, purchased by my mother for college graduation day and not used since, and Verandah, her finest dress, from the Somerville days. After mimeographing a jingoistic pamphlet directed against Reverend Mr. Davis and LBJ, a pamphlet calling them for what they were, racists and executioners, we departed in pairs for the church, where Davis was to preach on "Making God Real in Your Life." We were received at the door with a nervous cordiality by the good congregation, which included an unusually high proportion of generals, congressmen, and government officials and an unusually small proportion (about six) of blacks. In short, our Inconspicuous Garb did little to disguise the fact that we lived in Washington, D.C., and not in Chevy Chase and were freaks to boot. We were out to deny Lyndon Johnson his last sacred refuge and whatever remained of his sanity if we could, at the risk of arrest, which was little enough to fear for people in our situation.

Well, the LNS building itself must have been tapped, or else we were quite unlucky, for Johnson didn't show. (It had long ago been certainly established that the phones were tapped, so we never discussed the upcoming church thing that way.) But, what the hell, there was still Davis to put down, and when he began to preach, we threw the whole scene into an uproar by rising from all over the church and leafleting the pews. At first some people thought we were *ushers* or something as they grinned broadly while accepting the leaflets. But soon there was a steady, angry hum in the air which grew to a roar when Mike Lucas (Mike was into Marcuse, Brown, and pansexuality, ask me to tell you about him some day, a really far-out guy) began to leaflet the sanctuary choir. We were unceremoniously ejected from the church, of course, Mike going out on the shoulders of six male ushers, like a corpse, and all of us lucky to avoid getting clapped in jail. The last thing I remember is myself and V calmly speaking our rehearsed legal lines ("Are you asking me to leave? Are you authorized to declare that I am trespassing?" and all the while leafleting) to ushers who were ready to bash our heads on the nearest available cross.

As far as I could tell, and I watched the Monday morning papers very carefully, Lyndon never went to "his" church again, at least not while we were in business across the street; and he suffered all kinds of tepid abuse at the hands of more human ministers in suburban churches. And some congressman introduced the incident into the Congressional Record, calling us "adult hippy-beatniks" and blasphemers and all, and more or less suggesting life imprisonment or deportation. So the little differences our presence made in D.C., small incidents like the theater and the church, gave the Washington Free Community some import and significance after all, even if our message was essentially negative rather than joyful and aspiring.

One final thing about that January was the Jeannette Rankin Brigade, a coalition of three thousand ladies who came to Union Station to protest the war to their Congress, to "petition for redress of grievances." Miss Rankin was the first congresswoman in American history, noted for voting against both world wars. The trenchant point about her return to Washington as a dissenter, I thought, was that Congress hadn't even *voted* for the current war, but nobody mentioned that. The scene was thoroughly stolen, for me, by the emergence of the Women's Liberation lobby among the group, which argued that the *real* issue was male chauvinism, the historic slavery of women to men, the unjust reduction of women to basically servile roles (such as "wife and mother"). I agreed with most of their arguments, but when the Liberated Women threw me out of the room, shouting "Oppressor!" and stuff, I felt a lot like a white liberal getting unwelcome at SNCC, and it felt pretty lousy. But Verandah and Miss Katz told me afterward that *they* didn't feel oppressed (like to see some man oppress those two), so I concluded that the Liberated Women were a bunch of dikes, and so much for that.

❊   ❊   ❊

One other thing happened in early 1968 which deeply affected all of our friends in Washington, and most of our friends all over the nation. Bob Dylan emerged from two years of silence with a new album, *John Wesley Harding*. We fell asleep during "I'll Be Your Baby Tonight" every night, usually minutes before the Q Street Squealers started their sunrise cacophony in the treetops. Wesley Harding, "a friend to the poor," saved us from the dreary world of systematic revolutionary effort and brought us all the way to Vermont, and did as much for dozens of our dearest friends. There is no way we can properly thank him. And there is nobody who can make music like Bobby Dylan makes music, music to change the world. You will, of course, know the melody to "The Ballad of Frankie Lee and Judas Priest" already, but consider the words just one more time:

> *The moral of this story, the moral of this song*
> *Is simply that one should never be where one does not belong.*
> *So if you see your neighbor carryin' somethin',*

Help *him with his load!*
An' don't go mistakin' Paradise for that home across
   the road.

✶   ✶   ✶

From LNS 34, January 29, 1968:

PARADIGM, Latter Section of Long Poem THESE
STATES

These are the names of the companies that have
   made money from Chinese war
nineteenhundredsixtyeight Annodomini fivethou-
   sandsevenhundredtwentyeight Hebrew fortythou-
   sandsixtyeight postMagdalenian
These are the corporations who have profited mer-
   chandising skinburning phosphorous or shells
   fragmented into thousands of flesh-piercing nee-
   dles
and here
listed money billions gained by each combine for
   manufacture
and here gains are numbered, index'd swelling a
   decade, set in order,
here named the office fathers in these industries,
   telephoners directing finance, names of Directors,
   fate makers, and names of the stockholders of
   these destined Aggregates,
and here are the names of their Capital ambassadors,
   legislature-representatives, those who drink in
   hotel lobbies to pursuade,
and separate listed, those who take amphetamine
   with the military, and gossip, argue, and pursuade
suggesting   police   coining   language   proposing
   thoughtstructure mapping policy, done for a fee
as troubleshooters to Pentagon, consulting Mili-
   tary, paid by their industries;
and these are the names of the generals & captains

*of military, who now thus work for wargoods
manufacturers;*

*and above these, listed, the names of the banks,
combines & investment trusts that control these
industries, & their highest lawfirms,*

*and these are the names of the newspapers owned by
these banks & persons*

*and these are the names of the airstations owned by
these combines;*

*and these are the numbers of millions of citizens
employed by these businesses named;*

*and the beginning of this accounting is 1958 and the
end 1968, that statistic be contained in orderly
mind, coherent & definite*

*and the first form of this litany begun the first day
of December 1967 concludes this poem of These
States*

Allen Ginsberg

CHAPTER FIVE

The seedy presence revealed!

We are reliving the last days of the movement; we are watching the movement die. Don't be alarmed—every winter has its spring. What we called "the movement," which started out as a peace-living opposition to slavery, racism, and war, has become an enslaving, racist, civil war of its own; in short, it died. Many of the people still active in the new movement are in reality dead men, killed off by bitterness and frustration and the unceasing attention of your television cameras. But many others have made the transition from the dying thing into a new living alternative which is trying once again to save the world—save the planet, in fact. This New Age defies our attempts to put it down in print; "no sound ever comes from the gates of Eden." So you and I, dear friend, are pounding the streets of New Babylon for the last time, clearing Three Thomas Circle out of our systems, reliving the awful assassinations; we're closing the book on the 1960s, and good riddance to all that striving after wind.

Here's a lesson I honestly believe I learned in my lifetime: ideals cannot be institutionalized. You cannot put your ideals into practice, so to speak, in any way more "ambitious" than through your own private life. Ideals, placed in the context of a functioning business enterprise (such as the government, SDS, or LNS) become distorted into ego trips or are lost altogether in the clamor of daily ped-xing which *seems* related to the ideal but is actually only makework. It is possible, for example, to spend an entire day typing and transcribing and telephoning the words of Eldridge Cleaver without once considering their meaning, or feeling their strength. There are probably still some people around who are grateful for all the radical magazines being published, and believe they contribute toward social change, but for those who do the work behind the magazines life can be an unending succession of meaningless and disheartening chores which actually stand in the way of their own liberation. Thus LNS goes through ideological splits, the *Los Angeles Free Press* installs a punch clock, the *Berkeley Barb* becomes two warring editions, and everybody involved commits him/herself to a life of hassle and strife. And all toward goals which seem further away the closer we get to them—goals like peace and justice and freedom. Add to that what Paul Goodman called "the psychology of powerlessness"—our absolute frustration at being unable to change the world using the conventional methods of politics and violence—and it's easy to see why the underground press died too.

I am told that young people don't read anymore anyway, and that may be true. Most of *my* friends are reading more now than they ever have—books, not periodicals—as the stultifying Nixon years have seemingly given them all the time in the world to kill. They are reading Dante, the Bible, Kesey, Dr. Jarvis, Kerouac, Vonnegut, Shakespeare, Thoreau, Freud, Marcuse, Tolstoy, Chekhov, Eugene O'Neill, Melville, you name it. But the rock generation, now in its teens, doesn't read at all, I'm told, not even dirty books or underground newspapers. And it is certainly true that literature aimed at the young is a very chancy commercial proposition, as one paper after another folds and the kids have the good sense to bypass paperbacks purporting to be "hip" or somehow magically wise and with it. Stereo phonograph records, tapes, and movies are much better vehicles for speaking to the young. I myself, although no spring chicken at twenty-three, probably see three or four movies for every book I read, and listen to a dozen record albums.

There continues to be something of a young-writers group in this country despite it all, and I guess I belong to it in spite of myself. And LNS did provide a meeting-ground for young intellectuals in Washington; all whom I personally knew have since moved to somewhere else—the West Coast and New England, mostly. By the time the winter was ending, in February and March, 1968, the news service was drawing a great deal of its energy from such a group of writers, and most of its financial "security" from a group of wealthy and/or famous people who respectively made donations or threw benefits in our behalf. And thus we kept on keeping on.

Among the writers:

—Marc Sommer, 22, an earnest Columbus boy lately come from the cool detachment of the *Cornell Daily Sun* into the middle-class paradise called the Institute for Policy Studies ($50 a week, air-conditioning, and you don't have to *work!*). Marc went under the improbable pen name of Gaston St-Rouet, named after St-Rouet, Arkansas, where a plucky lad named Kevin Simptum was publishing, against impossible odds, a little paper called the *Fuckoff*. Marc went to St-Rouet and came back with some heavy stories about teenage vigilantes and the like. He also went to Hanoi and returned with stars in his eyes and even less flesh on his incredibly skinny frame. He had a Prince Valiant haircut and rimless eyeglasses and always looked and sounded like a graduate student in history at Harvard. But he was an impetuous dreamer as well, not one of your sober, academic types, and on Christmas he split for France with several hours' notice, to find a lost girlfriend. Marc's angular frame soon became part of the furniture at Three Thomas Circle, and in the basement laundry room at Church Street, where he and I went with Verandah for the express purpose of getting stoned. He managed to laugh a lot, a high-pitched giggle most welcome in our dire straits.

I last saw Marc marching in the anti-inaugural parade in Washington in January, 1969. He'd moved to a new commune in D.C. but had left the Institute—bit the hand that fed him by calling one of the professional lefties a pedantic old fart. And now he lives in Berkeley and does a lot of poetry, acid, and star-crossed fornication. Says he's happier all around.

—Harvey "Sluggo" Wasserman, 22, also from Columbus (the other side of town) was a Wilson fellow at the University of Chicago but with youth fare and all, was in Washington fairly often. His dispatch from the Fulbright hearings with Dean Rusk reappeared in *Time* magazine as an example of our biased reportage, and he has been grouped (in the *Boston Globe* magazine) with such writers as Goodman, Ginsberg, and Thich Nhat Hanh. I'm tempted to describe him as "irrepressible" or "ebullient" since in all my recollections he is laughing at the sheer absurdity of life. A splendid fellow and a smart-head, old Sluggo is now teaching grammar school (do they still call it "grammar school," by the way?) in New York City. Says he hates it and is moving to the woods.

—Craig Spratt, 19, lately of Nasson College's New Division in Maine, where he was made to leave because he smoked dope—an absurd piece of reasoning on any campus, rather like kicking somebody out of high school because his voice is cracking, but especially so at Nasson, where the entire student body of New Division was in those days stoned at all times. And everybody knew it. Craig comes from New Jersey, where his parents succeeded in instilling in him the most advanced case of generation gap I have ever encountered. Since leaving Nasson, and since LNS departed Washington, he has wandered around the East Coast, ending up in Boston more often than elsewhere, working from time to time and continuing his incredible polysyllabic raps to anyone who cares enough to listen—the story of his life, fully elaborated and viewed from many angles. Like the time he stayed five days in an Omaha motel attempting to convince a lady Air Force officer to marry him and eating take-out Chicken Delight from the local greaser joint. Or the time he pumped for inclusion of a critique of Stokely Carmichael by Phil MacDougal (white) in LNS and then fell asleep in the closet several hours before Carmichael Himself with five strapping bodyguards arrived in the office to threaten us. And who could forget his essay, "Sir John the Sincere," probably the most pornographic literature LNS ever published, to which *Logos* in Montreal gave over an entire page, but neglected to include Craig's by-line? Yas O yas, Craig is the born loser, the new generation's answer to Hart Crane.

—Mike Lucas, 22, was a refugee from Boston who had only one pair of dungarees to his name, and those with a gaping rip in the right knee. He found a home with Bill Higgs, the Mississippi lawyer who pulled us through one crisis after another, from which he was free to engage in guerrilla theater on the streets (e.g., staging the assassination of "MacBird" outside Ford's Theatre the night it reopened) and harangue us about the seminal importance of "Marcuse and Brown, Marcuse and Brown." Mike also espoused what he called pansexuality, which is the ultimate liberation; and which, judging from recent events, is no longer a shocking innovation of the avant-garde, but a conventional mode of behavior for successful rock groups. Hooray for progress!

Mike is lately involved with *Anarchos* magazine (and family) in New York, which Craig Spratt called "the great white hope for a while."

—Eugene Kahn, editor of the Bard College *Observer*, who worked for LNS as some kind of school-oriented journalistic internship, and protested from time to time that he *wasn't sure* about all this militant stuff. (He later turned out to be a pretty good egg and a mean hand at making stout tables for Massachusetts farm kitchens.)

—Hatti Heimann, an independent woman who had been involved in some tangential way with the Free University (later called Free School) in New York, and who seemed to me the classic stereotype of the well-educated New York-bred Jewish female whose deep intellectual commitment to social progress led her into the vicious arena of men's politics. An excellent mind and hard-nosed disposition took Hatti a long way. I count her as a guerrilla and true-blue friend. Last seen actively injecting her ideas into a chair-swinging SDS-PL confrontation in New York City, June, 1969.

—Bill Blum, mid-30s, formerly a State Department functionary, now writing a government exposé column for the *Free Press*, and the very picture of a mild-mannered reporter for a great metropolitan freak sheet—horn-rimmed glasses, crumbled sport shirt open at the throat, neatly-pressed slacks. He somehow retained his stuttering but unruffled composure through all the internecine scrambles in the *Free Press* office, and made his inconspicuous way through various government offices and committees faithfully gathering bits of information for some future use. And he's still doing it today. Sort of an I. F. Stone without the wisdom and inviolability which comes of advanced age.

—Steve Goldberg, 21, lately returned from a year as a Quaker aide in South Vietnam, and primarily devoted to the cause of draft resistance. Steve became our man in Chicago and his storefront apartment our Midwest crash pad. He is also conceded to be the most beautiful boy in the world, or so the ladies thought, and not one of them was unmoved by his charms. Now in Boston with a radical theater group and a Cambridge commune.

—Marty Jezer, 28, a pacifist buddy of mine from the Lower East Side (Bronx, originally) and habitué of 5 Beekman Street. Marty was a prime mover in *WIN* magazine which is still the most principled, intelligent, and entertaining magazine in the country in my opinion, and he is just now getting back into a passionate involvement with jazz which started somewhere in the fifties. He helped launch the famous Yellow Submarine for peace in New London, Connecticut, some years back and saved Josef Mlot-Mroz, everybody's favorite neo-Nazi, from drowning. ("He didn't even shake my hand," Marty mused afterward.) And he's now saving a little part of the world, in Vermont as it happens, from ecological destruction.

—Michele Clark, mid-20s, married to a New York City film-maker, and herself from the Bread and Puppet Theater. Michele has the longest, frizziest, wonderful brown hair and a throaty laugh. She was one of the many who hit Church Street while just passing through town, one of the few who stayed; and by the time she arrived in March of 1968, we were already talking about getting out. I saw my younger self in her face as she advanced all the arguments for our staying in Washington—guerrillas in enemy territory, keep an eye on the bastards, etc. After LNS split, Michele went to Cuba, where she met a man named Mungo, and then to Cambridge, Mass., where she taught school for a while. I don't know where she is now, but sure wish I did.

And there were many others. Some, like Aaron Frisch in New York, a middle-aged suburban housewife in New Jersey, a wire-service reporter in Vietnam, and an Army deserter in Sweden just poured information into our office without themselves taking by-lines for various good reasons. Others wrote regularly from lonesome and crowded outposts all over the mother planet. Unsolicited writing arrived in great heaps, and of course not enough of it was good in our terms, and some of it wasn't even accurate. We were not sticklers for accuracy—neither is the underground press in general, so *be advised*—but our factual errors were not the product of any conspiracy to mislead the young, but of our own lack of organization, shorthandedness, and impatience with grueling research efforts. *Facts* are less important than *truth* and the two are far from equivalent, you see; for cold facts are nearly always boring and may even distort the truth, but Truth is the highest achievement of human expression. Hmmm. I had better clarify this with an example: let's suppose, for want of better employment, we are watching Walter Cronkite on TV. Uncle Walter, who is cute and lovable and whom we all love, calmly asserts that the Allied Command (!) reports 112 American soldiers were killed in the past week in Vietnam, 236 South Vietnamese died in the same period, and Enemy (*not* Vietnamese?) deaths were "put at" 3,463. Now, I doubt the *accuracy* of that report, but I know it doesn't even come *close* to the *truth;* in fact it is an obscene, inexcusable Lie. Now let's pick up a 1967 copy of Boston *Avatar*, and under the headline "Report from Vietnam, by Alexander Sorensen" read a painfully graphic account of Sorensen's encounter with medieval torture in a Vietnamese village. Later, because we know Brian Keating, who wrote the piece, we discover that Alexander Sorensen doesn't exist and the incident described in *AVATAR*, which moved thousands, never in fact happened. But because it has happened in man's history, and because we know we are responsible for its happening today, and because the story is unvarnished and plain and human, we know it is *true*, truer than any facts you may have picked up in the *New Republic*. And the same kind of examples could be given for many stories unrelated to the war in Vietnam, all the way down to the dog-bites-man clippings at the bottom of page 38 in today's *Newark News*. I'm not saying it would be ethical to broadcast a false rumor that all bridges and tunnels leading out of Manhattan are indefinitely closed (though that might be interesting); but I'm saying that the distinctly Western insistence on *facts* (and passive faith in science and technology) betrays our tragically, perhaps fatally, *limited* consciousness of life. The facts, even if he can get them, will never help a man realize who and what he is or aspire to fulfill his natural role in the universe. Ain't it the truth? All we say: tell the truth, brothers, and let the facts fall where they may.

*   *   *

O K, I can see by some of your faces that I'm not going to get away with it that easily. But damn it you know the truth as well as I do, if you will but admit it. *Perceiving the truth* is something we all do naturally, can't escape it— it's simply the way you see the world, the relationship *you* have with the whole world around you. *Telling the truth* is more conscious, hence more difficult and unnatural. Most straight journalists, in fact most *people* in my country, see themselves in lifelong competition with other men for trifling honors and material goods, see life as one long quarrel with their neighbors, see themselves as masters of some men and slaves to others. This follows since most journalists, most people, leave their homes daily to go do the bidding of another, to remain in a place they do not enjoy and perform tasks they despise, thinking they have no choice. This is known, in an abuse of an otherwise beautiful word, as "work." And as such "work" eats away the larger part of their time and energy in this incarnation, they are lucky to accomplish anything they consider it *important* to do before they die. (The truth is only TOTAL LEISURE will allow mankind to accomplish all the things which *must* be done, and not total "work," as some poor slaves claim.) At any rate, we would expect journalists of this ilk (sometimes called "Working Press") to report *truthfully* as they see the world, but will they do so? Of course not, for they've compromised their right to truth as well as eight hours of their day. They will write serious accounts of the Chamber of Commerce dinner, the President's press conference, the Thanksgiving football game, millions of facts without even one simple truthful picture of the slavery of Everyman in "this dog-eat-dog world" they inhabit.

LNS and the underground press, in those days at least, tried to tell the world the truth as we saw it. The world is getting up in the morning around 2:00 P.M. Discovering opium. Having sex with somebody you just met. And your best friend. Longing for just an inch of honest black soil under your toes where you could raise one honest cucumber. Begging dimes at the airport (leave the bus station for the old drunks, respect their turf). Arranging the abortion of a child you're not sure you fathered. Bouncing checks. Getting stoned and meeting Christ. Getting busted for getting stoned and meeting Christ. Worrying about tomorrow the day after tomorrow. Splitting to Morocco. Getting all sick and strung out on Demerol. Tiring of your scene and leaving it. Trusting to God. Trying to be harmless and have fun. Tripping. Looking for a little sense, peace, or justice among powerful men and generally failing to find them. Looking to score. Playing music everywhere you go. Eating whatever you can get. And writing about everything that happens to you just as it happened.

*   *   *

We were accused of being financed by China, Russia, and North Vietnam; haw, haw. It is true I once received $25 from a man in Peking through a bank in Africa, but other than that we got money for survival from a very small group of people, mostly young, who'd inherited capitalist fortunes from their parents; from benefit concerts, plays, and lectures; and mostly from our subscribers, who were asked to pay $15 a month but seldom did. One barometer of our financial health is the LNS salary scale— ranging from $0 to $15 per week at its peak strength. Another is that our largest single contribution was $1000, and that only once. Removed to the farms, we can live quite well on just the sun in the morning and the moon at night, but I defy anyone to live pennilessly in the big city without freaking out, resorting to crime, or both. The cities, at least in this country, were designed to be nothing more or less than marketplaces; and he who goes to market without money in this vicious, self-defeating economic system finds himself rudely dismissed at every doorstep. I learned from repeated exposure to it that not even *jail* is free; in fact, considering the accommodations at D.C. Jail, the rates ($25 to $50 per night, higher for felonies) would make any ambitious hotelier envious. It is quite remarkable that "the movement" has gotten as far as it has with such feeble monetary backing, especially when one considers the astronomical sums the government spends on relatively less impressive projects. But chill penury combined with the urban marketplace environment has taken a visible toll on many of us. Bad debts continue to plague us. And, aside from acting out our lurid political fantasies (organize, rebel, overthrow), all we got out of it personally was some experience in the kind of Life of Constant Want which will soon descend on the entire nation as American currency and industry continue their steady collapse.

Among those who did gigs to pull us out of some debts was Dick Gregory, who deserves a whole lot more special mention than I'm giving him. It seemed this humane black man was always looking over our shoulders, from the day Marshall was ousted from U.S. Student Press in Minneapolis through press conferences at Three Thomas Circle ("Gregory for President Campaign Headquarters") and benefits in Maryland and Cleveland, to that hopeless Battle of Chicago. Laugh if you will at the image of white kids tagging after a black leader, but with Gregory there was no embarrassment, no unspoken or spoken barrier of communication. We had an honest relationship, allies through the skin. We weren't as close to Eldridge Cleaver, quite remote from him in fact, but I must add that Cleaver has the same fine qualities of candor and openness, that he is wise enough to assume nothing from the color of your skin, that you can, as I have done, talk with him in real terms rather than jargon or technicality. Which I, as a honkie, enormously appreciated.

And while I'm polishing off the topic of money (curiously mixed with remarks on black leaders) I want to fervently enjoin you, dear reader, to throw it all away. That is, learn to live without it as much as you can and we may yet save the world. "Learn to eat farther down on the food chain," your friend Keith Lampe says (that means more vegetables, fewer hamboogies). Plant everywhere. Give away what you can't consume. Don't under any circumstances accept the banks' new credit-card burns, Bank Americard and Master Charge, etc.—increased debt at 18 percent interest is no solution to inflation. Quit your job, increase voluntary unemployment so as to minimize the involuntary kind. Don't buy new anything. You really don't need air-conditioning this year. You really needn't make that flight to Denver. (You can walk anytime around the block, Dylan said that.) Plant flowers, vegetables, and trees and we'll all survive; buy McDonald's hamboogies every day and we'll all starve. Please, please believe me, I wouldn't lie to you.

*   *   *

Along about this point in our narrative, Eugene
McCarthy of Minnesota was running for President of all
the People and, in the queer victory-or-defeat terms of
American politics, getting somewhere, though not far
enough. His entrance into the contest had been Ko-rectly
analyzed by Allen Young in LNS as an attempt at co-
optation of the young, too little too late, and so on, and
thus from our political point of view he was no inspiration.
(I said earlier that "we" actually had many different political points of view, but none of us was "moderate" enough
to accept Eugene McCarthy. He wasn't for "immediate
withdrawal from Vietnam and self-determination for black
and brown peoples in America," was he?) More important,
he was the real enemy, we thought, since he was our competition for the hearts and minds of Joe and Susie College,
who were naïvely jumping on his clean-cut haywagon.
(Hum, they had to learn the *hard* way.) And his record *is*
dismal—voted for this and against that, blah, blah, only
very lately somehow got the spirit of brotherhood in his
blood. But I rather wish, in retrospect, that all those purely
political considerations had not so prevented me from lik-
ing him for, as politicians go, he's likable. And not nearly
the evil character that Bobby Kennedy was. (Why, B. Kennedy was *so evil* he called in Tom Hayden for consultation
a few months before he announced for President—talk
about co-optation!) (LBJ used to call Bobby "the little
shit," which you must admit says something for LBJ.) Anyway, and ironically, the closest thing we had to an ally in
the federal echelons became our worst enemy, and having
demolished him thoroughly in print, we set out to get Gene
McCarthy in person.

Here comes the U.S. Student Press Association
again. In the many months since we left it, USSPA had
been doing its best to get hip, in keeping with the movement toward the left on the Best Campuses, and thus
USSPA invited McCarthy, Robert Theobald, Jerry Rubin,

Abbie Hoffman, and us all to the same weekend conference in a large Washington hotel. Paul Krassner was there too, which ensured a zany affair, and a large cast of extras from the YIPPIE office in New York, the LNS office in Washington, and several guerrilla theater troupes showed up. Apparently, USSPA didn't realize the intense rivalry between the freaky-freakies and the Strip Clean for Gene forces, or else was misled by its wily conference coordinator, David Lloyd-Jones, a fun-loving Canadian who enjoyed playing with potentially explosive situations and with the funds of the *Washington Post* and *Newsweek*, which cosponsored the affair. The "membership" of the conference was a large group, perhaps four hundred in all, of college editors from all over the continent.

McCarthy was to speak on a Saturday afternoon in early February. That morning, little Stevie woke me with the news that he'd scored some acid. Heavy doses. And though I had always planned such things carefully in advance, and found impetuous tripping generally blasphemous, this time I just giggled and popped the tab. Started falling. Like floating down Alice's endless, painless rabbit hole sampling marmalade on the way. Landed in the picky rosebushes behind the house, with Stevie, calling up toward Max on the second-floor porch to come trip with us, shake hands with Gene McCarthy later. Now Max too, now Abigail. WHO will be next? Packed up a record player and stack of Bing Crosby 78s (Would you like to swing on a star?) and set off for the hotel. Immediately ran into Jerry and Abbie and Paul. Them too! Everybody in the world, it seemed, was tripping—except Eugene McCarthy. And that was *his* problem.

We set up the booth good Marshall had soberly planned to advertise LNS to the college editors in the plush lobby of the hotel and we turned on our record player. Soon Max and Abigail were performing a graceful and sweeping ballet across the floor, to the music of Mary Martin as *Peter Pan*. (It's not on any chart/You must find it with your heart:/Never Never LAND.) While Stevie went off to (successfully) pilfer office supplies from a nearby desk, I slipped upstairs for a conference with Paul and Jerry. Paul was sitting on the toilet and every time a particularly striking idea came into the conversation, he released a thunderous fart. In my condition, I recall, I found the coin-operated bed vibrator more remarkable than Paul's ability to so coordinate his intellectual and intestinal reactions. I don't think we decided on any course of action.

Downstairs, a cold debate on the war was going on. Those Opposed to the war had just spoken their piece, and the hawks were rising to begin a rebuttal when the lights went out. Ear-splitting noises came soaring out of surrounding loudspeakers—shrieks, blasts, the sound of metal against metal. Suddenly, a ghastly series of images—napalmed children, wailing Vietnamese mothers, cordons of bomber planes—appeared on three huge screens, Cinerama-style, above the heads of the astonished college audience. The whole thing went on for three or four minutes. It was an engineering feat worthy of the Nobel Prize, absolutely devastating environmental theater. And it provoked what was nearly a riot in the Sheraton-Park ballroom. When the films ended and the lights came up, a booming voice identified itself as Sergeant Something-or-other of the Washington police department, and placed everybody present under arrest for viewing unauthorized Communist films. Brought to you through a $10,000 *Washington Post* grant. Fists were flying in one corner of the room while Jerry Rubin stood on a chair in another crying "The YIPPIES did it! The YIPPIES did it!" The press dutifully wrote down "The YIPPIES did it," though it wasn't accurate.

General attention was distracted by a muscular young man wearing a conference name tag which identified him as editor of a small college paper in South Dakota. He was on a chair, shouting that he had been to Vietnam as a GI and the rest of us just *didn't know.* He was freaking out, he was clearly on the brink of something dire; he had internalized all the confusion and anger in the room and was its focus. Everybody stopped to listen to him. He was an actor from a Washington guerrilla theater group, planted in our midst, but nobody learned that fact until the next day.

Then somebody said Gene McCarthy had arrived, and one and all repaired to an auditorium to hear his speech. But Jerry had beaten him to it, and was on stage waving a copy of the *New York Post* which announced in 72-point type CONG CRACK JAIL IN HUE: FREE 2000. "People are FREE in Vietnam today, Senator, what d'ya think of that?" McCarthy looked confused and frightened, refused to answer. "It says here the Vietcong opened a jail in Hue and let out two thousand people. That's great huh?" McCarthy was nervous; "that's very nice," he stammered. "NICE! That's nice, he says," Jerry shouted. "Nice, nice, nice," came a muffled chorus from the back of the room. Other long-haired, tripping people went up onstage, myself included. I was wearing a bright-red Japanese kimono. I sat down next to Gene and opposite Jerry as McCarthy, faltering, began his speech. It looked, from the audience, like a Last Supper portrait with Clean Gene at the center of a long table lined with Martians, freaks, strange creatures who punctuated the speech with politically volatile remarks and obscene gestures. The audience came quickly to McCarthy's defense, but in shouting down Rubin & company, they also drowned out much of McCarthy's already hushed monologue. A few important questions were asked, but not answered; questions like "Do you advocate American withdrawal from Vietnam?" McCarthy could not be pressed by such extremist demands. But despite that, I had to give McCarthy credit—he was carrying on in an absurdly hostile environment, allowing the press to take photos which could only hurt his campaign—"Left to right, Senator McCarthy, Jerry Rubin, and unidentified persons who said they were from 'Liberation.'"

Suddenly, a muffled drumbeat filled the room. The wide doors at the back of the hall swung open and a bizarre funeral cortege entered, drummer in front and eight freemen carrying a large polished-wood coffin high aloft their shoulders. The audience, TV crews, secret-service men, and McCarthy himself began to freak out as the coffin advanced to the podium and came crashing to the floor, spilling forth an American flag and thousands of "McCarthy for President" buttons, the blue and white kind which had replaced Sigma Chi pins on campus. "It is the death of the two-party system!" shouted Mike Grossman of the *Free Press* as McCarthy mumbled "Thank you" into the microphone, turned on his heel, and ran, sprinted, fled up the aisle and out of the hotel. An NBC cameraman dropped his work and came racing over to punch out Mike Grossman, which he did. He was all red in the face and screaming something incoherent about our having defiled The Flag. Most everybody was unhappy about the whole day: the U.S. Student Press Association, which found its conference and its very organization in a shambles; the *Washington Post*, which disavowed the conference and swore never to donate money to USSPA again (nor, presumably, to *any* youth group, since USSPA was no SDS, and yet capable of such disorders); the hotel management, which wished out loud it had never allowed the conference to book in there; the college editors, who didn't get to hear Eugene McCarthy and write it up back home; McCarthy himself, who was visibly shaken by the contrasts between his young supporters and his young detractors, all white, all college-educated, and all against Johnson, yet susceptible to a kind of Generation Gap among themselves; LNS, which lost whatever foothold we might have achieved with the college press as a result of the backlash from my kimono; even David Lloyd-Jones, who (temporarily) lost his job. But I have to admit to a certain elation at the scene, in which the Rads did battle with the Libs and only the Rads were left standing at the end. McCarthy, who'd been sent on a white horse to salvage America, the Democratic Party, and the nation's youth, to prove that the country had another chance, had been vanquished by those he presumed to represent. And Jerry especially, Jerry alone, saw the whole thing as a tremendous victory for the anarchic life.

❈   ❈   ❈

There is no doubt that McCarthy had to be put down, that his timidity (vaunted by the straight media as "courage") and unwillingness to face crucial but unpopular issues had to be exposed. He threatened, after all, to tone down and slow up the movement of the national Head toward a true understanding of the war and of the disasters around the corner; and to some extent he succeeded. It's no credit to us that we handled our campaign against him so clumsily, but we did manage to lessen the numbers of young people entrusting themselves to his message. Some would argue that it's ultimately better to have Nixon (clearly reactionary, stupid, Chamber of Commerce mentality, etc.) in the White House than McCarthy (apparently liberal, somewhat progressive, and a poet— but no real soul for change), as Nixon polarizes everything and makes our side seem ever more virtuous and smart. Others would counter that McCarthy is a better-qualified man than Nixon to be president, hence would *make* a better president, and increase our chances of survival all around. I've never been able to make up my mind about that argument. I don't respect any politician I know of, so the issue doesn't trouble me too much. A plague on both their houses.

❈   ❈   ❈

My only other experience on stage with politicians was a panel I chaired in 1967, while I was still at B.U. The members of the panel were myself, Richard Goodwin, an advisor to presidents Kennedy and Johnson, John P. Roche, LBJ's "intellectual in residence," and Walt W. Rostow, believed most responsible for LBJ's Southeast Asian policies. Rostow and Roche, particularly, were awesome men who carried themselves with the air of power and authority—

abrupt, impolite, domineering—none of the gentle, confused qualities of Gene McCarthy. I made a speech demanding of Congress the immediate impeachment of Lyndon Johnson, for such and such constitutional reasons. Rostow urgently requested a glass of milk.

The draft was always a large concern around our office. A great deal of LNS copy was devoted to applauding those who resisted the draft, suggesting ways to get out of it painlessly, cheering on Dr. Spock et al. in the now famous Boston conspiracy trial. Most of us were members of The Resistance, which kicked off on October 16, 1967, with nationwide draft-card turning-in ceremonies (the largest of these in Boston, hence the locale of the "conspiracy") and has now largely vanished although more young men than ever before are resisting conscription, if my sense of things does not fail me. Just as I haven't wasted many words here reasoning my opposition to the war, I will assume that you, dear reader, are already energetically opposed to the draft and do not need a whole rationale to support you. The draft was most real to us as draft-age people, and no two of us chose identical ways to resolve the problem. Some were overage, some got deferments, some got off as drug-fags, Marshall got a C.O., and I tore up my induction papers at Boston Army Base.

I say tore up the papers rather than refused induction since I never actually went into the Army Base (except the year before, when I was leafleting there on behalf of the Boston Draft Resistance Group), and never took a physical. I adopted the attitude that the draft was not real to me, that I would pretend it wasn't even there, and in August, 1965, the twentieth anniversary of the bombing of Hiroshima, I burned my last draft card and signed off something I never intended to sign on to. I'm convinced the best way to deal with the problem is not to register at all; but, since that course of action was impossible for me, I thought the least I could do was refuse to acknowledge my draft board any of the power it claimed to have over my life.

After the tearing up of the papers, I went to Arlington Street Church with a group of demonstrators, and there the blueberry pancakes I'd cheerfully promised proved to be missing. But I think everybody had a good time anyway. And I felt especially good because I'd done something helpful to mankind—something that made a little bit of difference. For, you see, though time has made me doubtful of the *difference* which radical papers, marches, and organizations make in the world, I've always been absolutely sure that every man who refuses induction is one less man in the Army, one more on the positive side of the chalk line. Come what may of my little battles with the draft (two inductions and four physicals boycotted, a half-dozen FBI interviews in three cities, this specter of outlawhood over my head), I hope never to regret having handled it as I did— uncompromisingly but kind of cavalierly. It's something I'm doing, maybe the only thing, for my own self-respect.

*   *   *

Just after the induction thing, in March, I went out to Chicago to represent LNS at a select gathering called by Tom Hayden and Rennie Davis to decide what, if anything, the movement should do the following August during the Democratic Convention. Same old story—some thought no demonstration of any kind should be mounted (SDS leaders), others (Jerry & the Yippies) were coming to Chicago no matter what, and still others (Tom, Rennie, and Dave Dellinger) attempted to act as bipartisan camp leaders and bring all factions together. But when the shouting had subsided, nothing was decided. A small committee was formed, a Chicago office of National Mobilization to End the War opened, and thereafter Rennie, more than any other single force, organized the thing. Rennie was clearly *going* to organize it with or without a fruitless three-day gathering of movement types from all over, and no one can deny he did a good job of it. After the conference I retreated to Steve Goldberg's place, smoked up some delicious marijuana, and attempted to write some-

thing about the meeting which would make enough sense
to publish in LNS. Ended up wiring a brief and inconsequential story to Allen Young in Washington and going off
to see Bob Dylan's movie, *Don't Look Back*, which made
the trip to Chicago worthwhile. Got called a lot of names
on the street and threatened with removal of my testicles
in a restaurant, and began rethinking this Chicago thing.
Yippie?

✿   ✿   ✿

Back in D.C., it was getting high time to introduce
ourselves to the straight world. We decided to do that
through the hopelessly constipated custom of a press conference, which we announced with a bright leaflet head-
lined "The Seedy Presence Revealed!" And, indeed, the
"creeping presence" was galloping—to the point where the
straight media actually spent more space and energy on an-
alyzing the dissident culture than on any other single
"news," except perhaps the government. For, after the elections & the war, etc., and except for an occasional plane
crash or earthquake, we were the hottest news around. The
New York Times Magazine, in particular, has been carrying lengthy examinations of the movement in very nearly
every issue—and of course there is MGM's production of
Ché! O, well, if it sells they'll print it. We answered lots of
dumb questions from the Working Press, and got pretty
much what we expected in the next day's papers—dumb
articles. ("New Left Press Hums with Isms," the *Post*
said.) But of that came better articles, more sympathetic
and carefully written, in publications like *Time* and *Editor
& Publisher*, and out of those articles came subscriptions.
By March, the volume of our content and the number of
our subscribers had risen enough to force us to use a sec-
ondhand collating machine and pay a printer an hourly
wage to get the work through. (The printer, a relatively inexperienced apprentice, caught his hand in the gears of the
press and seriously cut several fingers. That's working for
wages.) But another result of the increased notoriety was

that people began calling us up for information about this or that, where *it* was *at*, etc. And of course we couldn't really help them.

My kind of life has been made immensely more difficult by the unceasing presence of the straight press, which comes around for motives of its own. You may be sure that by the time you read about something or somebody in the *Boston Globe*, its/his golden days are passed. Thus the media destroyed Haight-Ashbury, the anti-war movement, the underground press, and is rapidly getting to rock music. Speedy communications in the global village ensure that everybody everywhere will find out about every new project, and thereafter come to your doorstep seeking advice, approval, or sustenance of some kind; and, face it, most people are such schmucks you just don't want to meet them.

Last week, *Life* magazine came up the mountain, interrupted my bucolic utopian afternoon to question me as part of their nationwide survey of rural hip communes. Unh-huh.

CHAPTER SIX

Dr. King is dead in Memphis; the nation's capital ablaze

The very first night I stayed in Washington, while Marshall and I were employed by the U.S. Student Press Association, I could not sleep. So I went round the corner to an all-night laundromat in order to wash and dry the sackful of dirty laundry I'd carted all the way south from Boston. I'd settled down with a stack of tattered *Life* magazines and a *Post* bought from the sour delicatessen owner next door, whose store Elliot & I successfully boycotted for eight months as "unfair to people under thirty," and prepared to wait out my laundry cycle. I'd settled down, as I said, when in walked an old lady wearing a wrinkled cotton dress and white nurse's shoes and carrying coffee in a paper cup. She hobbled over to me and asked did I live around here?, and I said yes, just moved in today, and she responded in stentorian fury, stamping her foot, "GET OUT OF WASHINGTON! It's no place for a young man!" And proceeded to tell me the following story:

"Mrs. Lawrence" was born in New York but moved to Washington with her first husband, and had been unable to get out since. She had four daughters, three of them very well connected, married to professional men in Virginia, Albany, and San Francisco, and the fourth (whom she had by a black man) was a prostitute at a local hotel with two small children. This youngest daughter had just been arrested, and the children were missing. And Mrs. Lawrence herself had just been thrown out of her apart-

ment by her Persian landlord, a rat who wanted to trans-
form her quarters into a brothel. Moreover, she had that
day been mugged on the street and her purse stolen, and
the police (CIA, FBI, & local) were looking for her. And,
although she is a registered practical nurse, she'd been unable to get work for months. She was sixty-five.

Clearly unable to leave her there, and believing her
stories (which all proved, after exhaustive research, to be
true), I took her home. She moved into the room-with-a-
porch. She made tea, assaulted the young postman with
charges of having stolen her social-security checks, raced to
New York with the CIA in hot pursuit, confided in us little
secrets about ourselves and each other, said we would in
the end betray her. And so we did. Peter Simon, a brilliant
young photographer and friend of mine, drove Mrs. Lawrence, myself, and Barbara, a runaway, to St. Elizabeth's
Hospital in Washington one night, where we committed
her against her will. All appeals to her daughters and various charitable foundations had failed, and she had taken
over our entire lives. The hospital diagnosed her as having
acute paranoia and general confusion, mental imbalance.
Then, as now, I was far from sure which of us was crazy.
When she understood what was happening, the hospital
and all, she said only that I should get out of Washington,
or it would be the end of me. Since Mrs. Lawrence never
told a lie, I heard her words clearly for months after she
disappeared behind the hospital gates. I can still hear them
tonight. God Bless Mrs. Lawrence, she saved my life.

✻   ✻   ✻

Washington is the seat of evil in the world, at least
in our time. Those who direct empires of famine, torture,
and pestilence do so from that city. Is it surprising, then,
that the ordinary people of Washington include so many
cutthroats and thieves? Isn't it unfair to expect peace
(some would call it "security") on the streets of such a cit-
adel of murder and corruption? Of course it is, for the people know, even without schooling or indoctrination, that

their leaders have no morality worth looking up to; the people of Washington, who are mostly black, know without being told that all's fair in love and war, and that they must take what they can get, or be robbed of what they have. If we, as white radicals, comfortable enough in our *options* and our credit to live without robbing, expected to be welcomed by the people of Washington as friends and allies—and I think we did for a while—we were fools. We were no better than the Peace Corps creeps who move to D.C. for "a year or two" to start their careers; we were outsiders, transients. We could eat at Eddie Leonard's and some day laugh about it.

Verandah and I had bicycles which were functional in between the periods when they got vandalized by the people. On a certain night in spring, mine was working. I rode it home via Massachusetts Avenue, a well-lit boulevard graced by new hotels and office buildings (such as the National Rifle Association and the Australian Chancery), a street I'd often walked at three or four in the morning. A sports car with two people in it, a white man and his wife or girlfriend, was stopped at the Scott Circle traffic signals waiting on a red light. From nowhere came a group of young black men. They dragged the driver of the car from his seat and the woman from his side and began to beat them on the ground. They kicked and punched him all over his body. I put the bike into high gear and got out of there without a second thought or a word.

Everybody back at the house heard my story rather calmly. Most of them had been beaten on the streets, and the incident was neither unusual nor shocking to them; after all, a man had been killed around the corner just a few months back, and bus drivers (mostly black men) were killed nearly every night over a few dollars in fares. And, under normal circumstances, I too would have been blasé about the massacre on Scott Circle. "So what? So that's Washington," I had often said. But this particular incident seemed to break me. My so what?s became an elaborate analysis of the reasons for crime—fruitless crime,

crime in which the mugger or slayer gets no more than fifty cents or a dollar in material returns—in Washington, and the reasons why it was ungovernable. The people of Washington, I finally realized, *know* that the Empire is dying; and they speed it to its death with burning and rape. They have every reason for reacting in this way, and those who publicly condemn them and strive to put down the emerging civil chaos are the same ones who are responsible for it. But what place is there for us, white foreigners in a black city, in this revolt? None. Prolonged residence in Washington was going to send us, eventually, to the very government and police we despised, for protection against the real enemies of the state, the indigenous black population. We were to be the victims, not of any noble struggle for liberation, but of the violent spasms of a dying regime. We were living in the heartland of death and failure, incapable of either reforming the decaying establishment or dealing it the final blow. We'd probably die in the gutter, victims of a chance assault by someone in need of expressing his frustration and bitterness. I longed to be a Flower Child somewhere where there was light and hope, and not shuffling through some dark and smelly alleyway in the last days of the Emperor's faltering city. I was scared.

✿   ✿   ✿

Dr. Martin Luther King, Jr., was never my idol, nor even a black leader whom I could respect. The black leaders I respected, for the most part, gave little or no effort to seeking acceptance or understanding by whites. Dr. King's credo of nonviolence was absolutely correct, I thought, in terms of ideals and principles; but that nonviolence, bound as it was with old-fashioned Christianity, seemed absurdly timid as a theoretical base for angry young black men, who formed the vanguard thrust of the black-liberation movement. But I could see that Dr. King enjoyed a large following among slightly older black people, and had the status of a holy man and a Messiah in black homes around the world. And I never doubted his sincerity in his own message and faith. So, when he was murdered in Memphis, I was angry and hurt: not angry like the young black people who'd had injury once more added to their insult, nor hurt like the old black people who'd seen their savior crucified: no crocodile tears like those shed by politicians and businessmen and writers of newspaper editorials whose lives are devoted to money and power and violence and against the ideals for which Dr. King lived: but angry and hurt at the boundless shittiness of white American humanity out of which I came, which had cut down a visionary black leader from whose crusade I myself first learned that all was not ambrosia in the world of my fathers. His death brought back the days of Medgar Evers and of Goodman, Chaney, & Schwerner—early days when I was still capable of profound outrage upon learning of the deeds men performed for hatred and spite. Now there was no shock or outrage, just a numb anger, burning resentment in my guts as I was reminded again that we are the most hateful, self-destructive nation of men on the earth.

What to do about it? Go to war? No, that *never* works, that's a primitive reaction none of us can afford. Leave the country then? Nowhere else to go—"one should never be where one does not belong." Pretend it isn't happening? Impossible. Hopeless, it was hopeless, there were no answers and nothing to be done.

Night fell. We were gathered in the office on Thomas Circle watching television and compiling statistics off the Telex of how many arrested in Detroit, how many killed in L.A., how much damage in Chicago. Clearly the nation was at war but the TV man spoke only of Washington, never indicating how bad things were up in Baltimore, thirty miles away, or anywhere else; and the newspapers of the next few days did the same, focusing on disaster in one area while largely blacking out news from other cities. Washington was to be the most furious battleground of all —surprising to most of us, since D.C. had never experienced even a fraction of the wide-scale strife which

wracked Newark, Watts, Detroit. We had offered the
building to SNCC as a headquarters during the insurrection, but SNCC never came to accept. We waited
for something to happen. I am sure a part of me wanted
the entire city of Washington to burn to the ground, with
all the Good People miraculously saved and all the Bad
ones dead or penniless. The image of a fat Texan fluttered
onto the TV screen—"mah fellow Americans, we are
deeply moved blah blah blah." We turned off the TV.

Hungry, but the stores were all closed, some of
them boarded up and others bearing defensive "Soul Place"
signs, like blood of the lamb. Found the Hotel Burlington
restaurant on Vermont Avenue still open and a crowd of
terrified white ladies and gentlemen eating dinner, speaking in hushed tones. Like French aristocrats fearful that
the rabble will break through their barricades, demand
their heads. We were cheerful, convinced that the worst in
store would be just deserts for Washington. Ordered something we couldn't afford (if we simply walked out without
paying the check, would they follow us into the street?)
and then complained when service was slow. Female restaurant manager, false eyelashes, was waiting on tables in
the absence of regular service personnel, doubtless black.
Cocktail? Just beer, thanks. Here are your fearless cub reporters dining at the Hotel Caravelle in Saigon, thoroughly
energized by the Tet offensive. What a story!

Back to the office. This is Friday night, April 4,
1968, and the streets of Thomas Circle are utterly deserted
for the first time. Sirens and tension in the air. The Action is
up 14th Street, perhaps five blocks away, yet no sounds
come from that direction. The office building is festooned
with posters of Malcolm X, Dr. King, No Vietnamese Ever
Called Me Nigger, etc., though there are no black people
inside. We assume that the action will move down 14th to
Thomas Circle before the night is over; we are not sure
what we will do when it happens, join in the fun we guess.
I have my eye on the plate-glass window of Eddie Leon-

ard's Sandwich Shop; I want that oil painting of the Bar-B-Q.

From the top floor of the building, it is obvious that something is coming down 14th Street, but it is not rebellious citizenry. It is a thick wedge of National Guard, armed to the teeth. They come in waves. They stop where 14th meets Thomas Circle and form a seal against anybody getting down that far. We are thus right on the edge of the carnage and with box seats. It is rather like viewing a parade from your uncle's apartment window right over the heads of the clustered spectators. We are the only building on the circle still occupied, and we are being covered from all directions, so that a would-be sniper, even a kid with a stick, would be picked off and shot down the moment he leaned out the window or over the roof. Nobody tries that.

By the middle of the night, it looked like the thing was not going to reach us at all and I decided to walk uptown and convinced Jan Wostmann, a *Free Press* photographer, to come along. I could not stand the tameness of my window-perch any longer. With our hearts in our throats, and press cards in our pockets, we set out across the circle, heading straight for that formidable line of guardsmen with poised bayonets. They proved to be both confused and bored and we got past them with a minimal amount of song and dance and headed straight up 14th after regretting-to-inform-them that we had no pot and couldn't help them in that department. A few blocks up 14th, the city lay in ruins. Cars were overturned, houses smoldering, litter and blood in the street, and of course storefronts wrecked beyond recognition. There were police and fire engines everywhere, but no people. Where were all the people? They had all fled to safer parts of the city, been arrested, or been killed. It seemed that the explosive action took place just after dark and lasted only a half hour or an hour, but that was enough. As in all true civil insurrections, the people vastly outnumbered the authorities and so for a time at least they went on their rampage unchecked by any real show of force from the cops. Then their work was done, 14th Street was demolished, and they moved on. And when there came to be fewer of them, the cops could risk beating those people down. I looked upon the scene with awe. A girl in a nearby apartment house leaned out her window and told me to go home, I was a white mother-fucker. I couldn't argue with her conviction, so I left.

The next morning, Saturday, martial law was declared in the city and a curfew was imposed from the hours of 4:00 P.M. to 6:00 A.M. The previous night's rebellion had been very costly, but worse by far was yet to come.

✿   ✿   ✿

Saturday brought tanks on major street corners and cordons of guardsmen everywhere. Tourists in the city that day would have found machine-gun nests posted on the steps of the Capitol and heavy artillery guarding the White House. We awoke to find a single-file line of Marines marching down Church Street, hup-two-three-four, with a stereotypical growling sergeant at its fore; so Marshall and I got out our Sgt. Pepper band-leader coats with epaulets and tails—they looked like props from a summer stock production of *The Music Man*—and we took our place at the front of the line and hup-two-three-foured all the way down the block, to the immense amusement of the enlisted men and the churlish fury of the sergeant. The latter threatened to shove our teeth down our throats, cut off all our hair, etc., etc., all the usual virility hangups. From there, we schlepped on over to the Institute for Policy Studies to see what us white radicals was gonna *do* about this riot situation, to attend a meeting of the Committee for Emergency Support (for the insurrection, that is) called by famous grown-up area rads like Arthur Waskow and Andrew Kopkind.

There was much talk at IPS of expressing our solidarity with the rebellious blacks and so forth, but I could see that we were getting nowhere. After all, the rebellious blacks didn't need or want our support, it seemed to me, unless "solidarity" was construed to include shipments of guns, which we couldn't produce. The expression of solidarity which came out of the meeting got one paragraph buried very, very deep in a *Post* wrap-up of the day's riot action, and that was that. The best support we could offer, I thought, would be food and housing for those displaced from their homes, but we had barely adequate housing ourselves, and no food; and besides the liberals had already beaten us to it, as churches and government agencies all over town began dispensing cases of food and placing black people in temporary quarters, as often as not in the suburbs. The daylight hours brought enormous shipments of canned goods, coffee, cigarettes, bread, etc., some of which the Thomas Circle crowd unloaded on behalf of the Baptist church on 14th Street. Except for little services like that, though, we were obviously lacking any role at all in the drama—just a small band of white folks who were not afraid of rioters and had no stores to be looted, who in fact ardently wished they could join the fracas but had no way of proving themselves, and instead formed a goddamn *committee*.

There was plenty of work to do back at Thomas Circle, printing up dispatches of Friday's deaths and destruction, answering phones and so forth, and I found myself still there when 4:00 P.M. rolled around and the curfew went into effect. The question then was whether to observe the curfew, thus cowing to a totalitarian, unconstitutional law, or to risk arrest by crossing the street and getting some food at the Baptist church. When we got hungry enough, the decision was made in spite of ourselves. Marty Jezer, Craig Spratt, and I went over to the Baptists without incident and had a reasonably filling meal while we picked up the latest gossip—somebody had indeed broken into Eddie Leonard's, somebody else got People's Drug Store, eighteen people were dead tonight, six thousand had been arrested, the downtown shopping district was being hit hard. Satisfied with our visit, we picked up two people from the *Free Press* and set out to cross the street again and return to work on Little Johnnie, the press that wouldn't quit. But this time we didn't make it. Stopped by a couple of fat patrolmen in a cruiser. I knew the scenario by heart and was already considering who to call for bail, and how to protect my glasses. Didn't we know there was a curfew? Yes, but we just went to get some food. Never mind that, you dirty creeps, the curfew etc., etc. Yes, but we're *press.* We know all about your press. Let's go.

The paddy wagon stopped several times to pick up new passengers before we arrived at the precinct house, where several thousand other prisoners were being held. There was the usual routine, gimme your wallet and glasses and belt, hey you've been here before, you don't *learn* do you? I was learning. They put us in a one-man cell, eight of us together, including seven freaks and one old black man who told the following story: "I's goin' to work and the man say, 'You got a PASS?' and I say, 'I ain't got no pass, I don't need no pass,' and he say, 'You got no PASS you go to jail.' I's goin' to work is all." There was one steel slab and we took turns sitting on it. Otherwise we stood or sat on the cold concrete floor. There was a toilet but it didn't flush and it was full from the previous night's inmates and reeked of the worst smell I've ever experienced. Up came the Baptist food. Night passed and turned to day—we could tell by the faint light through the guards' doors. Hours passed as they released one cellful of men at a time. They released us at a rate calculated to spill the last man onto the street just as the curfew went into effect again. The noise, the smell, and our exhaustion were overpowering. The lieutenant in charge refused to return my glasses until I got a State Department lawyer, of all people, to complain about it. Later, I. F. Stone called us to register his outrage at professional journalists being arrested for curfew violation, but I didn't have the strength to make an issue of it, and moreover couldn't accept the premise that professional journalists should have any privileges over ordinary folks. Went home and went to sleep.

When I woke it was not Sunday, but Monday. Lost

a day there somehow but it wasn't the first time such a thing had happened to me so I wasn't overly bothered. There was an air of occupied Paris in the house. The curfew was in its third day, I learned, and there were still no signs that the city was returning to its usual "calm." The hup-two-three-fours had been replaced by armored tanks around the corner from our house. It was already past the curfew by the time I arose and for that reason, and because Verandah had scored where many had been burned, I decided to make it a holiday from Liberation News Service. But no such luck—there was this and that and the other thing to accomplish down on Thomas Circle and we had to risk the curfew, had to, had to, I was told. We would go in the hearse, I heard, Marshall and I and Marty Jezer and Bill Robinson would simply *drive over there* in the hearse, through the riot, after curfew.

  Let me explain:

  "In the hearse." Marshall and Verandah and I were considering a trip to California; we had the idea that we would meet all or many of the underground newspapers we'd been corresponding with for lo these many months, and even produce LNS on the road. For such a project, we needed a vehicle and neither Marshall's tiny green Triumph (GREEN POWER) nor my dilapidated Chevrolet (NELLYBELLE), which burned oil and got its driver arrested, would suffice. So Marshall found a 1950 Cadillac hearse, owned by a Princeton University student, and for a small sum wangled himself a month's trial driving on it, after which he was, presumably, to purchase it. It was a florid statement on something, all shiny and velvet and enormous, just the thing for a Dadaistic trip to California and back. Driving it under these circumstances, following Dr. King's death, made us afraid that the local people would interpret it as some kind of cruel joke, and Washington in those days was damn poor humor. But Green Power was indisposed, so if we were to get to the office at all, it would be in the hearse. Walking was out of the question.

  "Verandah had scored where many had been

burned." That afternoon, before the curfew fell, Verandah was at home alone and was visited by several youthful pushers from Dupont Circle who had an ounce of dynamite grass for sale. Never in my experience in D.C. had a salesman come to our door with such wares (it used to happen in Boston, though). We'd been approached on the street a number of times and each time we bought it turned out to be a placebo—in other words, hay. What a *burn*. But this delivered-to-our-door stuff was truly dynamite, outasite and all those other adjectives reserved for highly potent shit. Without considering the peculiarity of the situation, for indeed *everything* was peculiar then (to quote Alice), VP called Marshall at the office for advice—should she purchase a "birthday present"? Yes, by all means she should. So she put forth her "salary" of several weeks, which amounted to $15, in exchange for the ounce. It is important to realize that, at the time we decided to drive to the office in the hearse, we had been smoking this stuff for an hour.

"Bill Robinson." Bill was a skinny kid from Antioch or Oberlin or one of those freak schools in the Midwest, very soft-spoken. He came to LNS, like Gene Kahn, on some kind of school vacation; and he left right after the curfew was lifted. I thought I'd never see him again but ran into him in Greensboro, North Carolina, in March of 1969. I was speaking at the University of North Carolina's symposium on the New Left, and gave up my room in the redneck booger motel to move in with Bill in his small walk-up apartment; fantastic guy.

In our stoned condition, then, we decided to venture forth into the unfriendly night in the hearse. Marshall had called some lieutenant at some precinct and gotten assurance over the phone that our metropolitan police department press passes would be honored after curfew; and even though my metropolitan police department press pass had been scornfully dismissed two nights before by the arresting officer, I climbed into the Cadillac hearse, carefully secreting the stash under the back seat in order to stone everybody over at Thomas Circle when we got there.

There was a fifth person in the hearse—Allen Bloom, Marshall's businessman brother from Denver, who had the misfortune to be in Washington that night and insisted on being taken to the airport so he could get *out*. This projected trip to the airport added another rationalization for leaving the house and risking the street. Poor Allen Bloom really needed help; he'd just sat through several hours in our living room in which marijuana was smoked before his very eyes (he wouldn't touch it himself) *and* Marty, just for a goof, burned a dollar bill practically under his nose. This last stunt, invented by the Diggers some time ago, had a remarkably adverse effect on Allen, who was so visibly alarmed when we threatened to burn twenty dollars that we had to reassure him we were only *kidding* already.

We set out into the evening. There is a cloud of smoke over our neighborhood and strange noises in the air. We are stopped at the first street corner by a puzzled National Guardsman. We show him our metropolitan police department press passes; "working press." We just happen to look like Venutians and be driving a hearse, is all, and we're going to WORK. He lets us through. Next street corner, same business. Third stop, 16th and Q, three blocks from the house, we run out of gas, and there are no National Guardsmen or police cruisers, just two friendly-looking unmarked Volkswagen bugs. As everybody knows, VW's have Good Karma. The nice men in ties and shirts identify themselves as leading members of the Narcotics Bureau. I find this very funny. I am stoned. We show them our metropolitan police department press passes, but they very politely inform us that these will not suffice for after-curfew activities. Marshall mentions the lieutenant at such and such a precinct. They reply that said lieutenant never authorized our voyage in the hearse. We are arrested once again for violation of curfew and the omnipotent paddy

wagon magically appears from around the corner. I am getting so well known at D.C. jail, I think, they should give
me a permanent number and cell, like Ted Williams's shirt
number on the Red Sox. The team of experts goes to work
on the hearse, searching it without a warrant, until they
discover what they presume to be narcotics. Marty and I
are accused of possession, since we were riding in the back
seat, while Marshall and Bill are simply in violation of the
curfew. Meanwhile, Allen Bloom magically vanishes in a
cab.

Down at the station house, and still high, I answered an incredible battery of questions by the police
officers, and declined to answer some others. I found the
whole experience fascinating, comic, not at all scary. Marshall and Bill were separated from us and thrown in with
all your common curfew violators (Marshall soon thereafter demanded to be taken to a hospital, claiming fatal
illness, and spent his night in the waiting room at D.C.
General), but Marty and I were given over to the
maximum-security felony block. This cell was paradisal
compared to the last one we'd shared—it had a working
toilet and a steel slab for each of us, and they served
Spam-and-oleo sandwiches at dawn. We couldn't complain.
At one point during the night, I was taken in for finger-
printing and mug shots, all that sort of thing, and the po-
liceman in charge of the print operation was black. He was
also charged with filing the "marijuana" for future use as
evidence against us. While printing me, he carried on a
chuckling rap about what a *dumb* honkie *I* was for getting
caught with that *little bit* o' shit, and how he had it *six
inches deep* in his foot locker in the Army, and never got
caught. "Oh, yes," I defended myself, "it may be a *little bit*,
but it's DYNAMITE!"

Two and a half months later, when the case came
to trial, the charges were dropped. A pale and wan Narc in-
formed our lawyer that they couldn't find the evidence.

But of course we didn't know at the time of our ar-
raignment that it would work out so smoothly. We knew

only that the judge was fat and greasy, that he roared "Journalists? These guys look like they came out of the gutter in Georgetown!" and so forth. And, even after the rebellion was over and the city back to normal, there were police with teams of dogs on our corner and cruisers and wagons everywhere. The police force was shortly strengthened to 4400 men in a city of 800,000, which gave Washington the highest police-per-person ratio in the country. And we were the enemies. It turned out, for example, that while Marty and I were enjoying the special charms of the felony block (we befriended a man named Stony, who had been given eight years for armed robbery, which he performed because it made him feel like a KING, the top banana, to hold up a liquor store, and he walked down the street feeling *so* good), Craig Spratt was being arrested on the other side of town. And Craig got himself into a large cell with several hundred black guys and only a half dozen white ones, and escaped by moments the same kind of pummeling, jaw-cracking, fracturing beating which the other white guys got; the bailiff saved Craig from the emergency ward. But on the other side of the world, in San Francisco, Marshall Mitnick, one of our dear friends, was in the same situation and got multiple concussions and burns. One of us was *always* being either mashed by the people or arrested by the police at all times, it seemed. Small fortunes got thrown away on bails and fines. It was crazy, it wasn't even heroic or funny anymore. There *had* to be an easier way to overthrow the state!

A friend of mine named Schweid goes up for narcotics trial in Salt Lake City this week; when he left the farm he explained to me that people who get busted, at least our kind of people, always "cop a bust." That is, they invariably *want* to get busted, or consciously step into situations which they *know* are foolhardy. Schweid was busted once while climbing into a locked window in Ann Arbor, Michigan, and again while gambling in Las Vegas—"copping a bust." He may be right. Certainly we could have avoided the narcotics bust by simply staying home, or at least venturing out *clean*. Just by remaining in Washington, where we could be so easily singled out, we were copping busts. But for a long time we felt we had to *prove* that we could take it all; I'm thinking of a night when Marshall, tripping, went out into the streets wearing only his Moroccan robe and shower thongs, carrying a feather bird on a spring, like Diogenes looking for an honest man. Asking for it. I suspect the same syndrome affects dissident young people all over the country: people copping busts everywhere. But that isn't to diminish the fact that most of the busts are repressive and unfair, if not obscene; that narcotics busts, especially for grass and acid, are actually *political* busts, used against those whom the establishment has reason to fear; and that black people do not have to cop busts, too often black people get busted *because* they are black.

       ❄   ❄   ❄

Martin Luther King was dead and where did that leave *us?* When every other reason for leaving Washington made impeccable sense, we would fall back on the argument that the black people, after all, *had* to stay there—as if we had made some inviolable pact with the black people not to desert them. Now it became clearer every day that we were no use at all to the black people in Washington; we had no part in their struggle and no material help to offer. We had few friends. Almost all the news we published was out of New York and San Francisco and Boston —why not relocate in one of those places? There would be like-minded people, all kinds of stuff going on, local richies to hit up for occasional donations. We could leave Michele Clark in D.C. as a reporter of government and demonstration-type stuff, since Michele was hot to stick around.

The days were growing warmer and we could feel that blistering summer coming on. Something had to be done fast, we had to find a new home. At the same time, we had to pick up the pieces from the riot, reconsider our alliances with black-power stuff: should we leave it alone? Did we have a right, after all, to even talk about it? And there was the trip to California, would we ever get there? The hearse was now out of the question. And there was the mounting, awesome debt; we owed every utility company in town, plus bills of various size for rentals, paper, ink, presses, etc., etc. And in the midst of everything, things at the office were not going well—a serious personal rift between Marshall and Allen Young was widening and getting more hostile. Liz Meisner had split to Berkeley, resigning from the LNS board with observations like "the house on Church Street attracts freeloaders like FLIES" and "the LNS mailing list is carrying a lot of dead weight." Indeed, our subscriptions were up to five hundred or more, but we all had to agree that the vast majority of underground papers were not worth reading—not merely because the printing and art were so bad, but more because the content was banal, illiterate, or jingoistic. Confusion filled our heads. We knew we were in a bad place, but the odds seemed against our ever getting out of it; we'd become a stagnant filler service for a lot of fourth-rate publications, we'd done some eighty issues without a rest, we all hated each other, we were all hungry and overworked to the point of exhaustion, we were frenzied and mad.

And Dr. King was dead, A. J. Muste too, also the San Francisco *Oracle* (which stopped publishing) and Boston *AVATAR* (which was taken over by a splinter group different from the original editors). Any fool could see by then that the future of the "movement" was in coercion and violence, wars and propaganda, and not in beauty and truth. We were almost beaten.

Easter came. The cat, Keats, had kittens in a closet.

Verandah and I kept Easter vigil in the basement, considering all the weighty problems I just summarized for you; considering how our lives had been given over to slavish routine and mindless tasks, wondering how we got *there* after starting out on such a noble, idealistic level. We thought and thought about it. It was one of those magic times when answers just come to you, when you suddenly see your way again after being lost in the darkest night. I had last felt this way in Czechoslovakia, when I could see Liberation News Service coming into being. And when you get that feeling, when you decide what your next cosmic project toward saving-the-world is going to be, it's simply a matter of ped-xing to go out and *do* it; all the future rests, for me, on these occasional moments of inspiration. So we kept our vigil, as I said, until the word *VERMONT* popped into our heads, almost simultaneously. Vermont! Don't you see, a farm in Vermont! A free agrarian communal nineteenth-century wide-open healthy clean farm in green lofty mountains! A place to get together again, free of the poisonous vibrations of Washington and the useless gadgetry of urban stinking boogerin' America! The Democratic Republic of Vermont!

Well the idea didn't come out of *thin air*. The combination of LNS and Washington had pushed us to the brink of something drastic; and our ecological sophistication told us that the cities and everybody in them were doomed. "Don't drink the water and don't breathe the air" is pretty sound advice these days in the places where most Americans live. If we have to be poor, we said, let's be poor in Vermont, where God will give us at least half a chance to raise an asparagus or a cow instead of merely raising rhetorical dust. Let's go somewhere, like Vermont, where you can rise from your penniless bed in the morning without fearing the sights and sounds outside the door. It was decided. We'd learn to survive *and* begin building a political state, a nation, where free men could live in peace with their brothers. If we could build a news service, why not a nation? It was decided, too, and some months earlier, that LNS should move to a farm; for with all its information coming in via phone, Telex, and mail, there was no reason why the news service shouldn't thrive in some rural township. Marshall and I had carried this notion to the point of searching for farmland in the Blue Ridge Mountains of Virginia, but the prices for moderate plots of land were in excess of $50,000 so we had to abandon the whole idea. But Vermont land wasn't worth such prices, in fact it was some of the cheapest land left in the country; and could the mortgage on the farm possibly be higher than the inflated rents we were paying on the house and office? O God we had the *answer!*

I had to tell somebody about this fantastic decision, about the solution to all our ills. Marshall wouldn't do, he was freaked enough already with trying to solve financial problems, resolve his differences with Allen, and plan the trip to California. Allen wouldn't do, he was an incurable city-head, ideologically committed to the great urban nightmare, and besides he lived in another house, a cavernous haunted house at 12th and N. I decided to tell Marty. Marty was a pacifist and a cheery good man in general, and I knew he could dig it; and he did. So now Marty was with us, and what a spaced threesome we made! We danced around the stools at People's Drug.

> *No more D.C.*
> *No more D.C.*
> *No more D.C. over meeeee!*
> *And before I'll be a slave*
> *I'll be buried in my grave*
> *And go home to Vermont, and be freeeee!*

Now there was *really* too much to do. It was obviously going to take months of ped-xing to get LNS in such a shape that we could go to Vermont, and we just didn't have the time to spare. The Poor People's Campaign was due to arrive in Washington any week, though Dr. King's death had thrown SCLC's schedule awry, and it was important to maintain a large staff in town to cover it. (As it turned out, the PPC didn't get to D.C. until a week or so before we returned from the West Coast, so we missed none of the real flavor of the thing.) Our little seminars at the Institute for Policy Studies were in midstream. And the news service continued to make the sundry demands involved in three-times-weekly publication.

Despite it all, we *had* to get to California, both to

get out of Washington for a while and to find out just who and what we were dealing with through the mails. The view from Thomas Circle was so limited that we weren't sure there were even real people out there reading our stuff; what we had seen of them at the editors' meeting the previous October was sorry stuff and we knew there had to be better scenes going on. Besides, California was at that time the heartland of the movement, the seed of everything to come, the place where our friends, one by one, went to never be seen again. We, as much as Mr. and Mrs. America, were victims of a Disney-inspired vision of California as the Promised Land. We had an office in Berkeley which was nothing more to us than daily telegrams and the memory of an incredible stone in Cleveland. And we thought we'd better find out if LNS shouldn't relocate out there before jumping headlong into this Vermont thing.

So: how to get to California with no organization, very little money, no car, and multiple serious responsibilities back home. (This very dilemma may be facing *you*, dear reader.) Some people I know get there by bouncing checks, a system which has much to be said for it—it gets you there fast, and without the *tszoris* of all the crap in between East Coast and West—but it tends to catch up with you. Others hitchhike, a worthy if dangerous method which works only when you are alone, or at most with one other person, preferably female. What I did was to find the local U-Drive-It agency and get us a big new Mustang convertible.

It worked like this: in my country there are whole legions of people *so wealthy* that they travel back and forth between East and West coasts, and they like to have their expensive, comfortable cars to drive in both places. But they are *so helpless* that they cannot be bothered to drive the cars across country. So they pay your local U-Drive-It agency to find someone, *any*one, to drive their lovely mobiles across country while they themselves take an airplane (first class, I presume) and they rendezvous with their wheels on the other side. It's true. Now who would be

likely to want to drive somebody else's car across country
without getting paid for doing it? Certainly not tourists,
they drive their own cars; and not the bourgeoisie, they fly.
Not the very poor, they do not travel. That leaves the vol-
untarily poor hippies and an assortment of ex-cons, hustlers, and love-struck youths. Thus the U-Drive-It man
didn't blink at my long hair or my unemployed status, he
simply gave me a brand-new Mustang convertible, complete insurance policy, and a gasoline allowance. Now *anybody* can get to California!

Verandah and I packed the car. Marshall was back
at the office worrying about this or that important business
detail. Margie Stamberg, a reporter from the *Free Press,*
was to come along as far as Austin, Texas, where she would
work for the *Rag.* Though we were supposed to leave in
midafternoon, it soon began to get dark. Still there were
more details left unattended at the office. Allen Young was
to be in charge while we were on the road, and he had
Marty, Craig, and Michele to help him. The trip West had
already been postponed three or four times, and as midnight approached it seemed we must leave at once or be
forever trapped in Washington, never get out of the city
for the rest of our lives. I began to attach a holy significance to our getting out before the sun rose.

The sun started to rise. The black sky turned dark
blue. People were shouting. People were running. I took
Marshall by the sleeve and we raced downstairs into the alleyway. A fat rat crossed our path, vicious hungry city
beast. I put Marshall in the front seat, Verandah and Margie in the rear, and roared out the driveway without a
word. An hour later, when the sun was up for sure and for
good, and still no words had been spoken, we were in the
Blue Ridge Mountains of Virginia.

✿   ✿   ✿

(Hours before we left town, I finished printing up a
letter to my dearest friends, who numbered about sixty-five
at that time. I had something very urgent to tell them. In

the darkness of April night, I stuffed all sixty-five envelopes
into the little postbox outside Three Thomas Circle and
was myself a thousand miles behind before the letters
reached their destinations.)

APRIL 15, 1968: A LETTER TO MY FRIENDS

Great spirits now on earth are sojourning;
He of the cloud, the cataract, the lake,
Who on Helvellyn's summit, wide awake,
Catches his freshness from Archangel's wing:

He of the rose, the violet, the spring,
The social smile, the chain for Freedom's sake:
And lo! whose steadfastness would never take
A meaner sound than Raphael's whispering.

And other spirits there are standing apart
Upon the forehead of the age to come;
These, these will give the world another heart,
And other pulses. Hear ye not the hum
Of mighty workings?—
Listen awhile, ye nations, and be dumb.

John Keats, December 1816

Men are coming, great men who are among us now,
who will unite the extremes in to an unshakeable
structure, unshakeable not because of its suppression
of the will of the people, but because of its perfect
expression of that will. And from the present be-
wilderment, anger and chaos, a true will must arise
to replace that shadow of will, that vacant greed
which is now called the will of the people by the
clumsy dwarves who stumble where graceful giants
ought to strive.

Wayne Hansen, *AVATAR* 22

If you swing with Bruckner, you'll find out where
salvation is really at.

W. D. McLean, *Le Chronic* 3

Dear friends,

For some time, our shit has been coming together. I
suppose it all began when we were born, most of us being
rather young; but very probably it began before that, for
we are all products of events as well as of ourselves. The
war in Vietnam brought a lot of it out, most of us being
American; it brought to us a sense of the urgency in our
movement and thus served as a valuable catalyst for our
growth—our recognition of forces which were there to
begin with. It has something to do with the schools we at-
tended, those cottoncandy emporiums of the fifties when
Elvis Presley outsold Dwight Eisenhower on the charts and
those ferociously self-contained universities where we
fought for recognition as the acned, anarchic, but sensitive
human beings we were. It has much to do with the civil
rights movement, on which we indulged ourselves in the
early sixties, and the black insurgency, which is painfully
and beautifully real on my street tonight. And it has to do
with that portion of the "hippie" movement which is in reality a new Dadaism. For some time, our shit has been
coming together.

The single force which made this country tolerable
during my growing-up years was The Movement, a term
and a group which have come to have less and less meaning. At one time, The Movement was easily recognizable as
the people on the bottom of the ladder, suffering the most,
who wore SNCC buttons (black & white hands clasped)
and believed that John Kennedy was not the *entire* American dream. People in The Movement were warm & good to
other people in The Movement, as well as to people in general; they were funky, informal people who dressed poorly
and would always share the humblest of personal belongings. It felt good, it felt right, it felt holy to be in The
Movement. *This little light of mine* . . .

The Movement died long before Martin Luther King died, but he was a symbol and his death has an air of finality about it for The Movement. What we now call "the movement" is actually a thousand movements with a thousand inhibitions and restrictions and interpersonal hangups to it. (This doesn't mean, for example, that I am upset by Black Power as a separatist movement; to the contrary, I find it inspiring and necessary. But I am irrelevant to it.) What started as a small group of people (we could always tell, for example, who also smoked pot among us, and we kept our secrets from the "straight" world), easily recognized, has become millions upon millions. The "local organizers" have organized no localities. The anti-war movement (in its hundred variations) didn't end the war; worst of all, though, the anti-war movement (formerly "peace movement") has been slowly co-opted in the public mind by profoundly pro-war forces—Kennedy, McCarthy, businessmen, etc., people who do not disagree with the morality of murder but who see *this* war, *this* time, as unproductive.

I do not seek to reconstruct the original movement, because I think we have all learned from our mistakes and I think our original optimism, our expectations for reform in the nation, would be hopelessly naïve today. I seek to rediscover, however, the joy and the purpose that movement held, and to apply them toward a revolution in life, *my* life, *your* lives—not the lives of any silent constituency for which we speak. The revolution is *us*, the revolution is *now*; the revolution *had* to happen, we didn't simply *devise* it in order to keep occupied. And the revolution is necessary, bloodful shitspewing agonized plastic saccharine shallow world that we live in makes it necessary for survival, for survival.

It all began to take shape, at least I first noticed it, maybe five years ago. Do you understand me? O we recognized the shallowness of America—later to recognize the brutality of it, which till recently we had not personally felt. America is shallow because America is frozen food and better ketchup bottles and lousy theater and boredom,

boredom. America is brutal because her boredom is unper-
turbed by slaughter and torn tender loins, raw flesh is her
meat. America is beyond repair, America must be destroyed as an identifiable entity, and humanity replace her.
America is a *granfalloon*—a gathering of people under some
title which makes no sense. Which of us is so foolish as to
be proud to be born in America—as opposed to anywhere
else? What the fuck difference does it make? You are my
family, you are the people on whose consciousness level I
feel, you are not a *granfalloon* like America or the Boy
Scouts or Harvard University or Students for a Democratic
Society.

It all began when Doug Parker designed the flag—
black flag! O mankind's vivid shadow!—for the *B.U. News,*
which expressed in graphic form what the flag expressed
silently; when Verandah Porche opened the hovel in Somerville which Richard Schweid slept in (with various
ladies); when Don McLean started the Yankee Independent Party (YIP) and Jerry Rubin, some months later, the
Youth International Party (YIP) and both of them *really*
wanted to get to Inscape, to personal liberation, to turn on
in peace; when Allen Ginsberg proposed a map/collage
of Constipated America in all its aspects and I went to work
on it, astounded by what I saw; when Phil Ochs offered the
pleasures of the harbor; when Don McLean almost
dropped out of B.U. and almost into Inscape; when I
dropped out of Harvard, sighing relief; when *Avatar* said
"Hey, Governor Volpe: UP YOURS!;" when I realized I
should re-take up what I dropped when I stopped playin'
the pianah; when Marshall Bloom made an epic out of a
greasy-spoon diner on an acid trip; when Elliot B chased a
honeybee.

Now, in a time of great crisis, in a time of
bloodshed and agony and stupidity, in a time when men
read and write only to believe street signs and pen death
warrants ("the hand that signed the paper felled a city"),
in a time when history is remarkably dismissed, in a time
when the future is so uncertain, in a time when men have

so many resources for peace and creativity and a money-
less, workless, governmentless society and a place so
beautiful and so eager to be inseminated:

In this time, in this place, brothers and sisters, we
gotta get our shit together! we gotta write together, paint
together, sleep together, have children together, study to-
gether, build together, love together, publish together, play
together, make music together, say YES YES YES together!
we gotta, we gotta, we gotta! the time is ripe and the fate
of everybody of everybody of everybody hangs in the bal-
ance!

Yesterday was Easter morning, and Verandah and I
slept in the one bed but simply talked through the night.
When the sun came up, she made breakfast and I investi-
gated Keats' new kitties. The black one, the black one
pouted at me then OPENED its eyes for Easter. Opened its
eyes for the first time and stared at me, the beautiful little
black one, as if to say "I'm ready. Are you?"

Just before I went to Czechoslovakia, Thorne
Dreyer and I were sitting with thirty-five others in an
apartment owned by the editors of *Viet-Report* magazine.
Each person was asked to explain himself. Thorne said
only: "I'm the editor of the *Rag* and I'm ready." I'm ready.
I'm ready. "Ready for what?" I asked. I'll never ask again.

For some time, our shit has been coming together.
How much longer, Lord? How much longer before we
wind up together, snug as bugs in a rug, in that Inscape to
which we are unerringly pointed tonight?

peace & freedom,

ray

CHAPTER SEVEN

Ped-xing all the way to California

[An author's note: Every self-conscious writer-fella worth his salt at one time publishes his reflections on traveling around the United States. Some, like Steinbeck, take their dogs while others, like Dan Wakefield, take a pocket flask and notebook. I took only my emotional hangups. The chief virtue of the following diary, I think, is that it was not written with publication in mind. Honest. The names have not been changed since nobody is innocent these days.]

i. Selma, AlaBAM

Selma, Alabama; April 19, 1968. By the time we had left Washington there seemed no further purpose to our leaving.

The Grand Tour of the nation we had envisioned complete with rock band, hearse, mimeo machine, and thousands of copies of underground newspapers had crumbled; our hearse became almost despicable after Marty Jezer and I got busted for grass on April 7 while driving through the black revolution, quietly stoned; the flailing neuroses of almost everybody in the Washington office kept us scared to death of ourselves and incapable of organizing Grand Tours; I suddenly realized that I wanted less than anything to go around talking *at* groups of people, and I really can't hassle underground editors (I either want to get *into* their families or stay the hell out); the D.C. rebellion brought on me a string of scheduled court appearances, one of which I've already missed; and I'm getting *drafted* again, for Chrissake. (Thank you, Holden.)

Anyway, I've been leaving Washington ever since I got there, almost a year ago, and probably years before that, while I was still in Boston. I'm sort of looking for a home within America and trying to be so damned conscious of my needs, requirements, interests, what I'm *looking for*. The happiest I've been to date has been in the looking.

I'm searching for love, which I peculiarly think will require geographical exploration, and I'm trying to escape from myself. I've been notably unsuccessful. This journal opens in Selma, Alabama, because I was moved by love found here to begin it; it could have opened in Grand Forks, North Dakota, or Durham, North Carolina, or Atlanta, Georgia, though, or a hundred other places I've been recently. I hope I don't wind up like John Wilcock, traveling for a living and sort of not belonging to anybody or not taking any small thing seriously because I've seen so much else, and it all melts into perfect human insignificance. (Although I don't know John well enough to say whether or not this kind of stuff has happened to him; he did wind up in New York semipermanently, 'cause nobody in his right mind is willing to say he's in New York *forever*. That kind of commitment would be wilting.)

Everything I have to say about America would be a commonplace and anyway everybody's been this route before (except me). In order to get into the mood for writing about "macadam plains" and stuff, you have to sit under a tree and think of yourself as Shakespeare or something. At any rate, like men's rooms and airports, highways are all the same all over—"one hundred per cent HUMAN interest," the sign says at the entrance to Selma, a few feet from where Viola Liuzzo was shot down. Selma, still, is less dangerous than Washington, D.C., if you keep your nose clean (i.e., don't try to solve other people's problems *for* them, don't express opinions, don't try to solve your *own* problems if your solution is communistic). Segregationists, I think, are different from racists and hard to hate because

they are such pathetic sick bastards: sitting around the
filling station indeed! Poor cracker mothafucker, nursin' his
shotgun, gonna take a pound of my flesh 'cause he's too
fuckin' stupid to react any other way, 'cause he's just an
ANIMULE! Unlike my friends in Boston! Unlike me! Unlike America! In the absence of *real* oppression in this
country, oppression that takes the form of human beings to
fear (rather than systems or the government or unemployment) these crazy white folk have to *invent* enemies: like
me, like me. I wish they knew that the threat my long hair
represents to their government doesn't threaten their trees
or lakes.

Passing a group of black prisoners on the chain
gang, we stopped to give them a pack of cigarettes. Natural
allies here, instinctive enemies in D.C. Jail; no tag on me
that says "white radical" in D.C. Jail, where Stony told me
of armed robbery and I sat felonized for grass and curfews,
and where my friend Craig Spratt, despite protestations of
support for black power, glorifying in the insurrection in
fact, nearly got the shit kicked out of him. Easier to
breathe in cracker AlaBAM than in the nation's capital but
impossible to stay here, impossible to stay. This great forest
is not the end of the line for *this* boy.

Betty Faye Barton of Selma took us in under cover
of night. Betty Faye thinks she's a wicked woman, wonders
whether her liberal sentiments (most liberal in town) are
sincere, dares to question, in hushed tones, the integrity
and soul loyalty of the dead Dr. King. Maybe, she thinks,
she's a kook—she *is* Jewish, you know, and that accounts
for some of that crazy rhetoric about the brotherhood of
man (always spoken with a habitual laugh in reaction to
the absurdity of the concept). Betty Faye works for the
welfare department even though her family owns a department store, which we presume has some bearing on Betty
Faye's strange profession of absolute equality of race.

Betty Faye worries about things, *thinks* a lot,
y'know? She never turns away folks who come to her door,
and she is gentle and kind in her loneliness, which she

knows is inevitable as long as she stays in Selma, which means forever. She wanted to come to San Francisco with us but retracted her wish-out-loud as soon as we eagerly offered her a place in our traveling van. She loved us and all the excitement we told of yet wondered at the last if we were "subversive." We earnestly replied yes, and Betty Faye sighed despondently, "O, I am so confused now."

ii. Stuck Insida Mobile

Mobile, Alabama; April 19, 1968. I had meant to go back and consider Durham and Atlanta, also to clarify some stuff about Betty Faye, except I am thunderstruck by Mobile. We stopped en route here at a gas station peopled by one elderly lady who pumped Standard Oil and sold sulphurized salt, and I felt a little like salt—you know, awful hot and thirsty (Dr. Pepper notwithstanding) until I saw the big ugly Atlantic—check, Gulf of Mexico—slimy and sunbaked, but wet and wide. It is a great consolation to know that U.S. 90 will keep us on that gulf all the way to Biloxi and New Orleans. The friendliest folks in Mobile, again, are the blacks. Mr. Albert Carl, janitor at the elegant Bellingrath Gardens outside of which, for lack of a ready two dollars, we are sunning, has predicted that Margie Stamberg and I will marry in San Francisco. Both of us kinda doubt it, 'cause she's only going to Austin.

Backwards now: Betty Faye and the East Coast. I hadn't meant this morning to shit on Betty Faye—to imply that she's unsophisticated or a secret segregationist or crazy. Most people in Selma are unusually candid and honest about their beliefs; Betty Faye, who is an intellectual, has to be confused and ambiguous in order to be *honest*. America has gone to her head while not her body (in other words, she's like the rest of us) and while we act in the context of Edward Albee and Upton Sinclair, she acts in the context of Carson McCullers and William Faulkner. Except, of course, it ain't ever that simple. Betty Faye is one of the best damn people alive in America, I know, because she *knows* how perverse America has made her and takes nothing for granted, nothing for inevitable. Betty Faye seldom leaves Selma and is properly scared shitless of Lowndes County, but she's been (once each) to New York and L.A., the latter place for a year, and she's more afraid there.

Atlanta is halfway between Washington and Selma both physically and spiritually. It sprawls around like D.C., has a liberal political outlook (Ivan Allen, the mayor, sells ink blotters and desks and tried to *lead* the memorial march for Dr. King by driving his car around to the front), has a lot of flowerpots (but very few real flowers or real pot), fat buses, etc. Tom Coffin and the other editors of the *Great Speckled Bird* are sort of the grown-ups on the hip scene, surrounded by much louder teeny types who still think they have the *right* to freak out (despite the city around them, which will eventually curb their *élan*). Like Selma, though, it has big homes and funky stoop-sitters and the *Speckled Bird* house, despite its metropolitan location, has two verandahs and a wooded backyard, all of which the editors have the refined sensibilities not to use. Atlanta is like Cleveland in downtown, like Washington in uptown, and like any seemingly secure, enclosed place behind its doors.

We spoke for a couple of hours with Miss Karen Edmonds, a poised black lady who politely runs (with Miss Ethyl Minor) the dead-quiet SNCC national office and holds down a part-time job typing and clerking for a group whose funds are provided by SCLC. Karen, too, was Atlanta-refined and knew the precise reality of her situation. Later, for a goof, I ate at Paschal's, black-owned and movement-famous restaurant, where Ralph Abernathy of SCLC was lunching privately in the back room.

Durham wasn't Southern enough to interest me and apparently doesn't much differ from places like Richmond and Charlotte, which have lots of industry and Northern flavor. It is only five hours from Washington, where we started, which is preceded by places like Baltimore, Tren-

ton, Newark, Wilmington, New York, Cape Cod, Boston,
Bar Harbor, and Packer Corners, Vermont, which last is
the best. But these places are not for a month's journal, but
a twenty-two-year-old lifetime of which I am bloody tired.
Except I took a vow in January never to go to New York
again, not again, and except for a weekend acid trip in
Jerry Rubin's East Village apartment, have kept it.

Marshall Bloom and Verandah Porche, the rest of
our party, have just emerged from Bellingrath Gardens,
Mobile, and with a last look at the Bellingrath Pet Motel,
we are off to the oily beach of Biloxi, Mississippi. V.P. and
Bloom, advised by Betty Faye to go to the gardens, talked
their way through the electric turnstiles with our home-
printed press cards. "There were all old people and families
with little kids," Verandah says, "and black people dressed
up like guards that look like they ought to be in jungle
dress, and that say stuff like 'Hello, Missie, did you enjoy
the grotto?' "

iii. The Saints Go Marching In

Lafayette, Louisiana; April 20, 1968. As luck would
have it (like the fancy novelists say) our party arrived in
New Orleans, without conscious design, the night of Spring
Fiesta.

We came to New Orleans from an inconsequential
beach at Biloxi, where I boldly changed into psyche-
DOOLIC trunks (bought for three bucks at The Rebel
Souvenir Shop) despite the barbs of the others, who were
all white, all male, and all in the Air Force. "Flower
power," they hooted. "Fuck it," I returned, and with Verandah walked (and walked and walked) into the
piss-warm Gulf Coast until every cracker-mother's son was
but a dot against the backdrop of the olive-green Buena
Vista Hotel. The reason they chose not to go into the
water, we discovered, had to do with its heavy concentra-
tion of slimy things that lived on! and so did I! The Air

Force guys later approached us with a request for some grass.

We left New Orleans early today, after a night which I half believe was a mescaline hallucination (except that we ain't tasted shit since Atlanta). I drove the car this dawn through Baton Rouge, Louisiana, on a highway that goes *through* the loudest, largest, most terrifying aluminum factory in the world, and having digested you, eliminates you out the other end ontopa a lofty, narrow bridge which I eventually figured out was crossing the Mississippi River.

Back to New Orleans: surely there must be some way of postponing the agonizing job of re-creating that manic-depressive city and our state. Everybody's gotta go there, gotta go, because you won't believe half the stuff that goes on, you won't believe so I won't tell you but the half of it. I go into all situations with certain preconceptions, y' know, and certain political and human convictions, and I look for people like me because, like the movement person I continue to be despite the not-so-recent death of The Movement, I *judge* people's worth as people. I admitted it, and I'm ashamed.

Anyway, New Orleans is supposed to be this family-entertainment version of Las Vegas, full of carnival atmosphere like in *Black Orpheus*, but integrated. A crock. New Orleans is carnival, but its carnival is true to its Latin roots, or *meat*, baby, *sin*. There was this mad parade with lots of middle-aged people dressed up like Madame de Sévigné and Lafayette and high school kids playing 1890s firemen (except one called to another, "Hey, what'd you get on your SATs?") and thousands of rhythmic spades carrying torches and swaying to the music of the Jefferson High School White Knights. The four of us danced a manic "When the Saints Go Marching In" on Rue de Chartres, getting into the uninhibited spirit of the moment and the place—*la place de l'église*. Blocks and blocks of iron-lace balconies, alleyways, shanty-houses, French restaurants: it is the work of freaks helping freaks for two hundred and fifty years. It has nothing to do with America, this *quartier français*, and its people are not Americans.

The funmakers are mostly over thirty here, the gay scene is peculiarly obvious (New Orleans' First: Go-Go BOYS), the CIA are everywhere they say. Jim Garrison is slightly teched, and the hippies aren't hippies but the present-day equivalent of juvenile delinquents who have substituted muttering "bad trip, bad trip" for "mothafucka, mothafucka." We tried without success to locate a local guru named Bill (old friend of V's from Somerville, Mass.) and got just as far as his Rue Royal doorstep. The "hippies" took us to a bar, their only hangout, where they cursed the cops, agonized the unavailability of grass, and engaged in bitter quarrels, frequently including petty violence. Rebels without a cause in a city too strange for even the most insatiable of freaky tastes.

The biggest and strangest mystery of the city is the spades. They smile meekly or shiver in abandoned rhythm as they drive the city's horses, torchlight her parades, shine her shoes, serve her aristocracy, play natives and funky decoration for the grotesque jazzshops and fleshpot halls along Bourbon and Basin Streets. By and large, public restaurants seem to be segregated by an apparently amicable agreement. No black was seen to have a peer relationship with any white, and yet, unlike Washington, New Orleans has not experienced what is commonly called "serious racial strife." Strife/life.

It was 3:00 A.M. when we left—Bill still missing and no offer of shelter from anybody else—although we were exhausted from the drive and from hours of plastic honky-tonkism. Hungry and lonely and sick of Orleans's tireless carnivalesque, we decided to head for Austin and find a beach or two to sleep on on the road (notwithstanding my geographical sophistication, which is adequate to inform me there are no beaches in the heart of Texas) and make no claim to understand the wild polarization of emotions we'd suffered in the French Quarter. Marshall led us to hot sugared doughnuts and black coffee, pissed once in the gutter, and headed West.

A city resident, drunk, had parked his car in the middle of the entrance ramp of the highway.

iv. Reminds Me of / The One I Love

Austin, Texas; April 22, 1968. There are many stations in life in which the residents will claim they hold the world, that there is no place out of ( ) which interests them as much as ( ) or is so important. I once felt that way about Boston and my friends who stay in Chicago despite its barbarisms claim that Chicago is "all there is." The same attitude is notable in Ann Arbor, in Berkeley, and in Austin, Texas. But in Austin, Texas, the local chauvinism makes a peculiar kind of sense.

If you lived in the heart of Texas, you would know that there is no place else. Texas is everywhere. It is at least two days' labor and two hot nights, even in fancy cars borrowed from uptight suburban Maryland chicks who are flying to San Mateo and need their wheels to follow, in order to get out of it once you're in. It is arid and flat and powerful, and it is forever. We may escape. If so I don't plan to return on the ground.

The University of Texas is comfortably equipped with head shops, libraries, an underground newspaper, a local Narc, and 90 percent of America's mescaline. We planned to spend a day and have spent two. Margie decided to stay. We were lost in the beautiful local fog of grass smoke and erotic overtures, and were lucky (in the rock-cold practical sense) to escape when we did. I had a night with Liz, who may or may not get out, who in any case is everywhere while being physically restricted to Austin, and Marshall was converted by an earnest numerologist. Verandah and I had pancakes and orange juice, then wrote zany postcards for two hours at the foot of the tower from which Charles Whitman shot down a dozen passersby.

The wall of the student union bears the warning: "The eyes of Texas are upon you." We did a dry gasp and kept writing.

Austin's underground paper, the *Rag*, was one of the first, and like many another, it is growing old. Its bureaucratic hassles, like ours at LNS, have become utterly and hopelessly unmanageable. But there seems to be no personality war going on, as the chief "funnel," Thorne Dreyer, exercises an authority which is gentle and decent. While Thorne and Marcelle slept, six of us (three transients and three stable, four male and two female) held an all-night Virginia Woolf session on the first floor of an old Longview Terrace house. Everybody was stoned out of his/her head, though, so the admissions we underwent, and the candid admission of the uncertainty of the future in particular, were almost painless. I drew a sketch and later sent it to a friend. Everybody's trespasses and sexual advantages-taken were combed. We looked deep looks at each other, she and I, but despite her assurances that "everybody fucks everybody in Austin," and his promise (directed at the visiting V, who was not interested) that he, the twenty-year-old hip cowboy, would surely fuck every chick in the nation, the emerging coalition crumbled with the sun and introduction of complicating elements.

When we decided to leave, still stoned, I felt I was passing up my golden hour in Johnsonland, but fornication never takes just an hour, and we might never have left. She promised to come to me in Washington, but, even if she does, it won't be in *this* world. She *is* the world within this special one, and could only be an awkward foreigner outside. When we decided to leave, still stoned, it was a shock to our hosts, who learned from the experience how easy it is to take up roots and go, especially when you're naïve about the road ahead. She stood on Longview as I saddled the Mustang (having packed the garbage) and handed over some good-bye presents. "You are beautiful," she said.

❋   ❋   ❋

We have been all day trying to get to El Paso over the green prairies topped with crew-cut hills. Barring automotive or nervous breakdowns, there will be enchiladas for supper late tonight or early tomorrow in New Mexico. Once free of Austin and its magic manyworld charms, all Texas roads lead, however lengthily, away.

v. Cheery Circumstances

Las Cruces, New Mexico; April 23, 1968. Texas becomes New Mexico gradually, although a formal border does exist. El Paso becomes Juarez, Mexico, with a bridge and a nod at customs. Las Cruces, thirty miles beyond El Paso, is like a mirror of thirty miles before. But the mirror is the desert, and the image a mirage. All that seems to be is not, and much exists for real under the surface.

Our friends Phil and Marianne Lynch live near the New Mexico State University in an adobe hut nicely fitted with electricity (cords stapled to the ceiling), indoor plumbing, and potbelly heat. Marianne, who will have a baby in five weeks, rules the tiny kitchen and brings in colors—red, green, yellow, blue—from Mexico. Tumbleweeds, cacti and poppies surround the mud-covered home and history books line the walls. It is peyote country.

Visitors to the hut include "Ruby" Jackson, swinger of a two-hundred-pound football player, black, who has managed to turn on the entire team to grass, rock, and Marianne's sandal shop, and Manuel, a brown liberation fighter. The roads continue to be long and straight, and the food in Phil and Marianne's home is exotic and delicious.

Paranoia miraculously lifted by all these cheery circumstances, then, I ventured forth this morning in search of fresh air in Las Cruces. We are exhausted and sick to death of being an obvious novelty and the object of some real hostility throughout the South and portions of the East. But the political and personal tolerance of Las Cruces is no greater than that of Selma. We are not, of course, run out of the town, but the university itself is clearly no rest-

ing ground and its students no allies. Later I learned that
Phil's job with the ministry on campus is threatened merely
because he *subscribes* to Liberation News Service.

Marshall made the point a minute ago that Americans are stupid: given enormous natural resources, they
still have not developed a decent or happy life-style. I realized how naïve it was (and is) for me to expect some fun-
damental philosophic differences between college students
(or cops) trapped in that beastly wall that is Manhattan or
quietly housed on the dusty prairies, under shelter of be-
nign sun and stars. Our little button, "I am the Americong,"
befits all the friends we've met on the way just as it does
not befit the others . . . things are just that polarized. Cong
or wrong? And I take Edgar Friedenberg's side (in his im-
promptu debate with Tom Hayden at Princeton) that he
would not submit the welfare and lives of anybody to a
democratic vote by Americans! If small things like out-of-
state license plates, the wrong accent, long hair, etc., make
us outcasts in our own country, there is hope left only if we
can get our shit together and begin our new communities
now—on the same land, the land which sits empty in
every state.

The only places in which we *are* acceptable—places
like the lower East Side, Harvard Square, Austin, Monte-
rey, or Provincetown—accept us because our numbers
make commercial sense. Our numbers make human sense,
too. I will not be human stuffing for Maurice Gordon's slum
apartments in Boston, nor window dressing for Chicago's
Cheetah any longer. New Mexico will belong to New Mexicans. And some of those empty valleys, forests, mountains,
oceans, farms, and lakes will be mine to offer shelter from
and to get a little work done.

vi. A Garden of Eden

Los Angeles, California; April 24, 1968. Uncle Joe
has lived in L.A. for twelve years and claims to like it.
Mike, inveterate hitchhiker and sometime Beverly Hills

gardener, does as little as possible and spends his days at the beach. John Bryan edits *Open City* and is committed to sticking it out in the Great Urban Center no matter how bad things get. Emmet Grogan is real. Jeff Kaliss got a job and thinks about leaving here and going back East but, as usual, is in debt (as he was, come to think of it, when he left Boston for L.A. in 1967).

> *California's a garden of Eden*
> *It's a paradise to live in or see.*
> *But believe it or not*
> *You won't find it so hot*
> *If you ain't got the do-re-mi.*

> Woody Guthrie

California is everything to everybody. Big cities, small towns, open fields as far as the eye can see, seashore and desert, mountains and valleys, forest and plains, sunshine and snow, famine and abundance, Mexican and American, black and white, right and left, and all extremes as well as middles, all beauty as well as squalor, all joy as well as pain, all calm as well as frenzy, all solitude as well as crowds, all love as well as, as well as hate.

Beach report. Water is moderately warm and conducive to orgasm when combined with mid-to-high eighties temperature here in L.A. and citizenry in various stages of undress. I'll have tomorrow's forecast right after this word from Forest Lawn, the mortuary that takes care of EVERYTHING.

Verandah's new dress. For a long time in Washington, D.C., little Verandah Porche had no money with which to buy a dress, and no place groovy like Design Research to steal one from. Marilynn had given her a black dress with ban-the-bomb symbols, but somehow the dress that was really Porche never turned up.

In this place, this time, I want to give Verandah a dress that will express her perfectly, and I know that there will be somewhere in this state a poet high enough to have made one which speaks as her poems do—candidly and certainly. When Verandah goes home, I want her to arrive in the dress that will bind her to me as sister and to the world as poetess and lover. That is what I ask of you, dame California, in your infinite wisdom and greatness.

vii. It's Never Really the End

San Francisco, California; April 27, 1968. And the monks arrived at Capistrano, at Carmel, and at the city of Saint Francis, to set right the godless natives of that place. No other place is so befitting an apocalypse, so defying the imagination to re-create that the author settles in for a bit to wander, watch, and consider.

viii. La Casa Cuesta Cita

Big Sur, California; May 3, 1968. Palo Colorado Canyon Road starts at the Pacific and ends in Middle Earth. Amid forest and hills and streams, the hobbits live and welcome you. Such a fabulously beautiful place cannot long last. La Casa Cuesta Cita ("house on the little hilltop") is an abandoned cabin, approachable only via a dangerously steep and soft path, in which live Chris Hawkins, fiddler; John, guitarist and former dope peddler; Margaret, you mourn for; Michael, flautist chick with long blonde hair who cruelly disappeared at dawn; Thomas Loves You, age eighteen now and carrying a bag of pet snakes; V Porche, lady poet; and myself. All of this is written away from La Casa Cuesta Cita; during our four days there, nothing was written although much transpired.

Some people who have come here stay for years, so many that the hills are full of invisible spirits at peace with the world. No census taker advances up Palo Colorado Canyon, no tax collectors at the door. The men and women of Big Sur are, nonetheless, not escapists. Their work in making something human out of something natural is difficult, yet joyous.

> You got to walk that lonesome valley
> You got to walk it by yourself
> Nobody else can walk it for you
> You got to walk it by yourself.

Middle Earth will break your heart, baby. After a while, it becomes clear you will either stay indefinitely or leave before it does you in. The comparison between it and the Old World is too cruel. Won't be long now . . .

ix. On the New Age

Marin County, California; May 5, 1968. In California, as in few other places, it is possible to live in the New Age without encouraging self-destruction at the hands of the Old. Although they are a minority even here, there are people who understand the absurdity of all that noise and gas which emanates from the cities and old-style mentalities; and, understanding it, they are free to reject it and stand apart in Kool Space.

—The Fabulous K picked me up on Coast Route 1, with a black chick named Betty White who did not hitchhike, but waited for the right vibrations to come down the road—for K. K is female, forty, has cropped red hair and sunglasses that wrap around her head, making her eyes invisible. K has a bag which contains Moroccan *kief* and electronic walkie-talkies suitable for freaking out the Highway Patrol via remote control, which she did. K intersperses her remarks with phrases like *"too much"* and *"farrr* out." And she enjoys wishing one a good day, Ray.

—Bala-Bala lives with a Mexican family at the foot of a mountain somewhere in Marin County, not far from San Francisco. The house was built by a member of the New

Age and is *full* of Kool Space. "Mommy, mommy, can I have a joint?" asks the six-year-old son. "Have you finished your homework?" Good food and quiet.

—The New Age is in outer space, outer space. Drugs (particularly well-considered acid) play a part in it, but a minor one when one considers the revolutionary dimensions of it all. It happens in your head, y'know, but has material effects as well. The New Age looks to the galaxies for further adventure and exploration, and utterly abolishes all racial, religious, linguistic, national, and cultural prejudices among earthlings ("humans"). The distinctions among men blur in the face of the great future before us.

If we live long enough to create it, the New Age will be *peace on earth.* The judicious strife we now suffer on earth must be related to and seen in the light of that Kool Space which will make it an ancient chapter in our development. At the risk of adopting missionary zeal, we ought to go back to the cities and bring out the young and the alienated, to the land and peace, "save" them in a sense from the death of the body and soul amid the glitter of better ketchup bottles and new Buicks.

The peace we find in Kool Space will give us the internal strength to move in the Old Age, in the cities, for example, without succumbing to it; the peace in the New mentality is a peace without adequate words ("notoriously non-linear these hippies," says the latest *New York Review*) and we should seek to turn on and carry away the prospective new people rather than merely convince them.

Free from material need, unconcerned for what used to be called "poverty," we will escape the poisons of the city, which itself inhibits our revolution and warps our art. The cities of America are unnecessary evils in an age of electronic communication and transportation; they will become hollow museums to our past, burned down by the poor during the last gasp of the Old Age and now echoing with the sharp footsteps of the occasional, amused visitor. There is Kool Space enough for all of us—*look up today, rather than down.*

This is a chronicle of our nights and days in California, U.S.A., which we now have left behind, tearfully but with full acceptance of the necessity of it all. We are now in Nevada, where we have been twice ordered to get lost while trying to buy a meal. They have atom bombs under their skin in Nevada and it itches awful.

I don't expect to come back to this place. Lucky Pierre Simon and Arty Marty Jezer, feeling the cross-continent call, have come to join V and me in the long trip home. Marshall got lost with an Indian tribe. Respectfully reporting from the desert, yr hmbl svt., R Mungo.

x. Just Can't Get Into It

Steamboat Springs, Colorado; May 8, 1968. There is a whole lot to say about San Francisco, Berkeley, etc., which I just realized I have left unsaid; so many scenes, so many that I just can't get into it. To say that the city areas of northern California are comfortable is to belabor the obvious; it is free city already, and freer country, although it has its seamy and its slick aspects.

The Colorado landscape has moved us abruptly from spring to winter, as we drive through snow and ice to a morning rest in Boulder. It will be, when we get there, over a thousand miles nonstop, except for Salt Lake City, which gets me into another rap.

In this mad pursuit of home within America, we find ourselves never alone, and Salt Lake City, even, reluctantly houses the young in transit (there being no young in actual residence). We met many freaks there, on the road, and in the combination café-bus stop, but none of them were Utahns—rather wounded folk and runaways, GIs deserting their San Diego bases for Canada, ex-students fleeing serious drug charges, outcasts and criminals and lovers and brothers. After some exchange of advice and solidarity, we went our separate ways.

xi. 100 Miles Per Hour

Omaha, Nebraska; May 10, 1968. The approach to
Boulder was through mountains peaked with snow and
coldly transfixed. There is a sense of permanence to them
that is rare—and which makes them more interesting than
all of eastern Colorado and Nebraska. Boulder is a college
town and has its share of New people, although those we
managed to speak with were of a slightly cracked sort. The
summer solstice is coming on June 21, they say, and with it
great floods which will cover five hundred feet above sea
level of the entire U.S. The only safe place, we were told,
will be the Rocky Mountains, and our freaky hosts seemed
somewhat crestfallen to learn that we had not come, as
they expect thousands to come, in preparation for the sol-
stice/disaster, and we were moreover going back East—
into the arms of Judas Priest.

Coffee and eggs on Boulder's College Avenue produced a nervous black cat who spoke this much true: he
does not expect the U.S. to continue to exist in its present
form beyond 1972. Scene shifts to a University of Colorado
SDS meeting, where frustrated kids talk of bringing the
University to its knees without getting themselves kicked
out! The issue is a golden calf—or bronze buffalo, life-size
—which the alumni have donated forty thousand needed
dollars to build. Scene shifts again: a campus coffee shop
and much talk of the New Age, Vermont, space, the mountains, mescaline, the police, the merits of life on this planet.

Nebraska now, and endless roads traveled in fla-
grant disrespect for the dignity of the locals until the
lake in Ogallala (home of the Sioux, now employed to
weave baskets for sale amid Japan junk at the white-owned
Sioux Trading Post) intruded on our Krishna consciousness. Until another flat tire, outside of Beaver Crossing,
brought help (at last) from Seattle folks en route to Europe
(making their way through acid sales), who gave us a
wrench and two joints laced with whoopee and left us to

blithefully wander. Until stopping in the utterly colorless Bonanza Hotel in utterly hokey, positively unbearable Omaha. Until we advanced to absolutely pastoral Iowa.

Muir Beach, California, where we dropped God's own LSD, and Meriden, Iowa, are one and the same now with a thousand other pastoral homes. Free of the city's corrupt hocus-pocus, we shall not want. We lie down in green pastures.

xii. Hogbutcher for the World

Chicago, Illinois; May 11, 1968. Hogbutcher for the world!

[The following two days were too awful to recall and the diary records nothing of them. Your correspondent vaguely remembers leaving Chicago under threat of having his balls cut off by an angry, gnarled middle-aged man on Michigan Avenue. Then, through the miracle of youth fare, he reappears in Washington, only hours before he is scheduled to depart National Airport for the North.]

xiii. This Aeroplane Has No Windows

Washington, D.C.; May 13, 1968. This aeroplane has no windows to the outside world. I am alone on this superlate aeroplane bound for Ithaca, New York, where I am expected to perform in front of a group of foolish people called the *Cornell Daily Sun* (a *granfalloon* if ever I heard one) for a modest fee. My actual interest in carrying through this latest in absurd assignments is to get out of Washington, having arrived ten hours ago and being ill at heart.

LNS has a new toy. It is a tape machine which answers the phone. Although intended for use when nobody is in the office, it can conveniently be used when you *are* there but can no longer stomach the phone. One gets to make funky tapes and turn-on prospective callers before one even knows who they are.

The Poor People's March began without us. The government says it has no money to give to poor people because it is "billions in debt" over the war. Says Jim Bevel: "You remember that JFK guy? He went walkin' around with hundreds of thousands of dollars in his pocket while people was starvin' to *death!*"

Starvin' to death, God I am starvin' to death. If this aeroplane doesn't get outta here soon, I may just jump off and catch another to the woods.

✿   ✿   ✿

Postscript: A Letter to Nel

Hello my pretty. Verandah here. Pierre has asked me to give you a rundown on the whole thing, but first I must explain that we all have different conceptions of the big move. Second, I must swear you to secrecy because we are all in flux and the whole thing is still up in the air, and we are trying to fix up the whole deal before we break the news. But being Pierre's lady and all that, besides being a pretty, and reminding me of my own self at age sixteen (except that you don't seem to have the crazies half so bad), you should be among the initiated. So brace yourself.

Our big friend Skinny Don McLean bought some land in the Green Mountain State last year and was the envy of his struggling pauper friends. That is some background material. I must get organized.

1. We are all of us city folk and, therefore, while being slaves to the hustle and bustle, we are susceptible to the bucolic myth.

2. Raymond, Marty (you don't know him yet), and I are all political freaks trying to be relevant, helpful, moral, revolutionary, forward-looking, virtuous, self-sacrificing, etc. (you know the scene). Anyway, I have been in the scene since grade NINE and miraculously, in spite of my most ardent efforts, the world has been getting steadily WORSE. For example, when I was first involved

with SANE (which was then considered radical) and the now defunct Student Peace Union (SPU) we were most concerned with disarmament and Ban the Bomb (etc.). Last week the U.S. tested the biggest underground bomb yet and it caused nary a ripple because people are too preoccupied with an issue called the War which has nothing to do with Vietnam, just a conversation peace that's rapidly becoming passé, like the chemise, and people have to find a way to end it because it's becoming such a bore.

BUT!! While Senior Citizens (anyone over thirty with many exceptions and some senior citizens underage) are dying of obesity, bad bowels, and ennui, behold there is a New Age of humanity bursting forth with cries of Oh Wow, Dies Irae, and FAR OUT! Space creatures, artsy-crafties, people who take themselves lightly and seriously, who think living is better than . . . what am I talking about, Nel—you tell me. The hippest chick I met in California was ten years old. It has a lot to do with post-psychedelic ethics—simply caring for your neighbors because there is such a tremendous universe to be lost in. It is acid consciousness but it has little to do with drugs. It's where your mind is at. But I am rambling far afield. Turn on, tune in, drop into Vermont.

We learned at Big Sur that the woods is it, the wilds, the ocean, the mountains are all IT! It is the place where you want to be. Precise as an arrow shot through a falling leaf.

To make a long story short, we're East Coasties so we're going to Do Our Things in the woods. Pierre's pitchers and poems and plays and new recipes and space-age clothes, hobbitses, hiking, painting, carpentry, films, MUSIC, BABIES, MERRIE FROLICKS, sewing circles, farming, nice animules, assorted debaucheries, you know what I mean. We can play croquet or go skinny-dipping in the Beaver Pond.

A Vermont farmer died last year and his widow is selling the land—a hundred acres with houses, barn, etc., etc. And as soon as we can fork up a little money for a mortgage, it's ours! The world is ours, or all we want of it. We're going to put out an occasional output called Work in Progress with everybody's good stuff. Pierre's photos, our plants, and animals and new babies. Verandah's new recipes and poems, Raymond's piano progress and plays WOW and little Nel's new film and lots more.

Raymond has a project to take over the world, beginning with Vermont seceding from the Union and having liaisons with French Canada. FAR OUT, baby, Far Out! More will be revealed in good time. But I'm tired of babbling so I'm gonna sign off.

Remember! You are deeply sworn to secrecy. Welcome to the New Age.

Love,

Verandah.

CHAPTER EIGHT

Doing the big Big Apple

Steve Diamond, a third-year English major and part-time journalism buff at Columbia College, was innocently walking down Broadway in New York City, making his way from school to his apartment on Claremont Avenue, which he shared with a beautiful girl named Cathy Hutchison. It was January of 1968. Passing David Cohen & Son's jewelry store near 121st Street, he saw a vacant storefront absolutely bare inside but for an exotic-looking teletype machine. On the door was a handwritten note which read, "Anybody interested in forming Student Communications Network/Alternative to the regular press, please call Jim Branigan at 534-2245."

So he did. "Right from the beginning, there was trouble in the house," he said. Jim Branigan wanted this new New York office to be a branch of the Washington-based Liberation News Service, but his partner Colin Connery wanted an independent operation out of the Big Apple; and Jim and Colin were moreover competing for the same girl. Apparently, Jim got the girl and Colin the New York office. Two days later, at a meeting in Steve Diamond's apartment, a Columbia Ph.D. candidate who'd recently dropped out of school and had an independent income, George Cavalletto, offered to become the manager of the new office, and got the job by default. The president of Union Theological Seminary donated the first month's rent on the Broadway office; you will recall that the Student Communications Network was intimately connected to the University Christian Movement at its inception. That night, some young enragé threw a cream pie in the face of a Marine recruiter on the Columbia campus, and Steve Diamond wrote up the story and sent it down to us in Washington. We laughed and authorized a New York City bureau at 3064 Broadway.

*   *   *

Allen Young regarded Columbia as his alma mater. He had edited the *Columbia Daily Spectator* there before going on to the *Christian Science Monitor, Washington Post,* and, ultimately, LNS. He'd also spent a few years in Latin America, where he filed stories to the *Monitor* and puffy things for the *New York Times* travel section in exchange for a little bread to live on. On a fine April day, he was heading up to Connecticut to speak at Wesleyan University, and dropped in on the New York office, which was close—both physically and emotionally—to the Columbia campus. He discovered that Columbia was being seized by SDS and several thousand followers. He stayed for the action. Tom Hayden showed up, too.

Steve Diamond had the story. Two photographers, Miriam Bokser, now sculpting in New York, and Kip Shaw, now farming in New Mexico, had the pictures. Steve Diamond cabled *Ramparts* magazine in San Francisco on behalf of Liberation News Service: did they want the story?

*   *   *

Marshall Bloom was sitting in Robert Scheer's office at *Ramparts* magazine in San Francisco. He was discussing with Warren Hinckle and Freddy Gardner (now, both, on different trips) an offer from *Ramparts* to house LNS in its new building in San Francisco, pay for our phones, and allocate us a small sum in cash every month—in return for which we would provide *Ramparts* with urgent national news for their new twice-monthly format. The whole deal sounded fishy to me.

Columbia broke in New York. Every television network wanted film and every magazine wanted stills from inside the occupied buildings. The only press inside was Liberation News Service. Steve Diamond had the story.

Marshall Bloom went to work editing it, adding to it, phoning everybody who had a phone, ped-xing the whole story under a tight deadline for the next issue of *Ramparts*. Warren Hinckle sat in his big leather chair and made demands —this or that be researched, this or that be rewritten, where the hell is this or that photo etc., etc. The nonstop pandemonium went on for days.

       ❂   ❂   ❂

Verandah and I were in Big Sur. Remembering Warren Hinckle and his demands, Marshall Bloom and the story-of-the-year, Allen Young and the heroic struggle Back There, the frenetic bidding by *Life* and *Look* magazines for the inside pictures, talk of an LNS book on Columbia Uprising already, we put out our thumbs with no particular destination. Left behind the spacy upper floor on McGee Street in Berkeley which we'd been given for housing, left it to Marshall Mitnick of the concussions and burns, suffered in the aftermath of Dr. King's murder. We were chanting to the pulsing rhythms of Christopher's fiddle and John's guitar. We were making the very moon quiver with our rapt music. "Listen awhile, ye nations, and be dumb."

Came the morning, I was awoken by two sheriffs rapping on the cabin window. They were not coming in peace. Still cloudy and confused from sleep, I found myself saying, without preconsidering: "Yes, sir, yes, sir, three bags full."

       ❂   ❂   ❂

Marty Jezer was in Washington wishing he was back home in New York so he could get ready to go to Vermont. *WIN* magazine needed him. With Allen sitting-in up at Columbia, he was so swamped with work that he couldn't even open all the mail that was coming in. And he hated Washington like poison. Say, how did he ever get into this position anyway? We called him up from Big Sur. Hey, Marteee! Why'n'cha come out to California, hey? We can all drive home together! Marty Jezer worked twenty-four hours nonstop on the LNS mailing, then got on a plane for California.

✿   ✿   ✿

Peter Simon, our photographer friend, was in Boston finishing yet another year at B.U. and taking pictures for the *B.U. News.* Miriam and Kip were already taking pictures at Columbia, and there was nothing going on in Boston. Peter Simon got on a plane for California.

✿   ✿   ✿

Bala-Bala, who had founded LNS with Marshall and me, woke me up one May morning in Berkeley. She was holding a fat joint which she lit and passed to me. It's the lost Bala-Bala come out of nowhere, finding me via vibrations! Can we be headed for *Ramparts* and another day of fat Warren Hinckle and the story of the year? No, we are headed for Muir Beach with Howard & Jane from the LNS Berkeley office, and Peter Simon too. Bala-Bala was an undercover revolutionary lady now, a lot of Eastern wisdom combined with a feeling for Latin earthiness and American sangfroid. Needless to say, a good time was had by all. After the beach, and after nightfall, we turned on Howard's FM radio, KMPX of course, and an unknown man named Dr. John the Night Tripper came zapping us through the speaker. "Outer space," was all he said.

✿   ✿   ✿

The Columbia story got filed and published in *Ramparts* and Marshall—we were fools not to have foreseen it —got lost with a bunch of Indians and was not heard from for weeks. His ped-xing successfully accomplished, he set to hallucinating again. That still left us in San Francisco and the office phone in Washington was now saying "This is a recording. There is nobody in the LNS office at the present time. At the tone, you may leave your message." We were hot to trot, freaked by all the awful possibilities of what was going on in our house and office back home, yet profoundly depressed by the prospect of the long East-bound drive. Peter and I found a U-Drive-It man and we were off to Chicago. There, V fell for Steve Goldberg's irre-sistible charms and Peter flew to Boston and Marty to New York. So I arrived back in Washington all, all alone. Craig Spratt was there and he took up the same conversation we'd been having the night I left. We went over to Thomas Circle and found it deserted; truly the only activity left in the news service was going on in New York, although the mailings still got miraculously printed and collated in D.C. I felt like Rancher Dude returning to Kittsville City, which he built from nothing, to find a ghost town. We played back the phone-answering device: "Beep. This is the Pitney-Bowes Company. Will Mr. Bloom or Mr. Mungo please call me at once regarding your postage meter. This is the fourth time I've called, Beep." We took off the phone message and made a new one, so that callers to LNS would hear Arlo Guthrie singing "Alice's Restaurant," followed by a series of aimless chants punctuated by Craig's imitation of a Top-40 Disc Jockey announcing, "From WASHING-TON! It's LIBERATION NEWS SERVICE! Starring LIT-TLE ANTHONY AND THE INPERIALS!" and so on. The first person to call and get that tape was Allen Young. He was pissed out of his mind.

Somehow May passed into June, the weather got progressively more humid and warmer, and all the lost people drifted home. Marshall reappeared with artifacts from his Indian period in New Mexico, including a pol-ished rock pendant which I wore about my neck until it, too, was stolen from the house on Church Street. Verandah came back from Chicago by way of Boston, bringing along Laurie Dodge, a New Age carpenter; but as they arrived at the house, they met a mystic (sleeping on our couch) who was heading for the Esalen Institute in Big Sur the fol-lowing morning. Remembering Chris the fiddler, Verandah looked at Church Street dimly, and she, Laurie, and the Es-alen freak were gone by sunrise, ped-xing all the way to

California for the second time in as many months. Allen Young returned from Columbia, but his mind was set now on moving the national office to New York, where there was excitement! people! and money! Since I was not about to defend staying in Washington, and farmland in Virginia was priced out of our reach, that left just Marshall to cling to the old homestead. Marty Jezer returned as well, for several trials related to our April busts. And Peter Simon took a job photographing for some fat-cat foundation in Virginia and moved into the basement of the house. Michele Clark moved into Marc Sommer's commune on S Street and Craig Spratt was always around, as often as not underfoot in the opinions of everybody except me. With my removal to Vermont pending just as soon as I could manage it, Marshall and Michele were the only really permanent people willing to stay in Washington, and the news service had grown to need at least a dozen full-time workers in order to maintain its established pace, and more if it was to grow.

The only other possible answer was for some of the New York office folk to move to Washington, but that proved impossible. They came down in George's car one night, had all their belongings stolen during the one hour in which they left the automobile unattended, and returned to New York the next morning. Nobody who was really ingrained into the Big Apple was willing to live in Washington, it seemed; D.C. seemed dull and stagnant and incredibly ugly to them. I had to admit that Bloom & I probably lasted as long as we did because neither of us *had* lived in New York for any substantial period, thus had no nostalgic memories of life on the lower East Side, upper West Side, or what have you. Like it or not, then, LNS was moving its national office to New York City.

Two people were sorry to see us go. One was Marshall himself, who (it must be recorded) maintained to the last moment that we could somehow find new people, new funds, and new projects without moving. The other was Bill Higgs, the Southern lawyer who'd given so many of his own years to D.C., who was energized and thrilled by our decision to locate there, who aided us, scraped up money for us, advised us, housed our reporters, wrote for us, and, from time to time, criticized us. I can remember sitting with Bill over coffee and Western eggs at the Trio Restaurant—in Bill's words, "King and Stokely and *all* those guys used to eat at the Trio"—and watching his face fall as I broke the news. A scant few months after we split town, Bill too hit the road—though I can't positively say that there was a causal relationship at work—and since then has been working for the Alianza Federal de Mercedes, Tijerina's group, in New Mexico.

The last thing that happened to us in Washington, the last *scene* we got involved in, was the Poor People's Campaign. After the April insurrection and all, I had more or less deduced that we'd be unwelcome around Resurrection City, but it turned out to the contrary—not only were white people accepted into the camp, but some of our furthest-out acquaintances came to LNS, in D.C., later in New York, and finally in Massachusetts, directly from Resurrection City. The oldest of these was Alex Kelly, a fifty-year old Scot who traveled the world around spreading cheer, and is now in Mexico or southern California; and the youngest was Lazarus Quan, Shining Youth, a seventeen-year-old high-school dropout from Florida who organized a high-school underground press lobby aided by, and within, LNS—sort of a Youth Auxiliary in a movement whose leaders were seldom over twenty-five. Lazarus has since forayed in Morocco, worked in London, and ended up back on the farm. Lazarus became the youngest person at LNS after Stevie Wonder was expelled from the house, following a stern lecture in front of our New York allies, for bringing heroin and heroin pushers onto the premises, and for general sloth; he was then dispatched home to New Jersey in the hearse, which of course he never brought back to its rightful owner until it was seized by the Garden State police boogers. God bless Stevie, he's dead now.

Resurrection City, you will recall, was a collection of A-frame houses which got quickly inundated in heavy rains, sank into the mud and a growing lethargy, dropped in population from a thousand at first to fifty or a hundred at the end (when government bulldozers razed the entire development), and provided a focus for at least a little bit of public hand-wringing over the truly desperate plight of the urban and rural poor in America. The chief problem at the camp was its leadership, which, lacking Dr. King's vital spark, failed miserably to impart any spirit or community into the campaign. Dr. Ralph D. Abernathy, who succeeded King, chose to live at the Albert Pick Motel rather than in an A-frame, which literally all the citizens of Resurrection City found hard to swallow. There were in addition a whole set of middle-class rules & regulations (no liquor, no drugs, no whoring) which were inimical to lower-class living; and though they got regularly broken, one was always *breaking the rules*, in other words, sinning.

Marshall got into the spirit of Resurrection City a lot faster than I did, and made himself a small cabin in the "rural" section, close to the California Diggers and Black Panthers. I found the bed there too damp and since we had a perfectly good slum of our own to live in, spent no more time down there than was circumstantially convenient. Needless to add, the Poor People were always getting busted for this or that (one man got a year in jail for carrying a penknife in the Smithsonian Institute), and by this time I was getting apprehensive about busts, and trying to keep clean until the narcotics trial was over. John Karr, our friendly attorney in the grass case, quietly suggested that— if it wasn't against our *principles*—Marty and I might consider getting haircuts before we appeared in court, and so we gave each other butcher jobs of a sort with a nine-dollar haircutting kit purchased at People's Drug. The kit was left to Thomas Circle when we departed with the express provision that it be used on people who were coming up in court—a good investment for the movement, we thought.

It came to be June 21, the day of the famous Poor People's March on the Washington Monument, a day when thousands of white liberals would fly into D.C. to express their solidarity with the starving. The UAW sent a large portion of its membership, and *AVATAR* sent two ace reporters, Wayne Hansen and John Wilton, down from New York. *AVATAR* had always been the best and most truthful of the underground newspapers, if it could be called an underground newspaper at all, in my opinion; and the Lyman Family, which lives on Fort Hill in Roxbury, Mass., had helped us out of quite a hole the previous December by sharing, fifty-fifty, the proceeds from a delightful benefit concert in Boston. After more than sixty obscenity busts and an interstaff split which took the paper away from the Hill people and gave it to a crowd of vulgar *left-wingers*, the original *AVATAR* group, Wayne among them, was down-and-out, both financially and in spirit. Marshall and I agreed that we'd do what we could to help out, which proved to be printing and paying for *AVATAR* number 7, published in New York in competition with the bowdlerized Boston paper. Since we had only our little offset press, we made it magazine-size, eight-and-a-half by eleven inches, and we printed five thousand copies of forty pages in four colors in a nonstop effort over eleven days and nights, then bound them with a saddle stapler borrowed from *WIN* magazine and distributed them five and ten at a time to newsdealers in the Big Apple, Boston, and elsewhere. It was truly a labor of love for John Wilton and me, but I've still not lost faith in the final product. I had intended to reprint Wayne's essay, "A Sermon Made in Latine, And Tales of Amazing Adventures in Washington D.C., the Nation's Capital," at this point in my story, but I can't bring myself to take it out of the context of the entire issue of *AVATAR*, with its photos and crazy type, and even the ads. Some old issues of *AVATAR*, which is now defunct in printed form (they are making movies and records), as well as issues of the *San Francisco Oracle*, the early *San Francisco Express-Times* (new called *Good Times* and substantially different), very early *Ramparts*, and Vancouver's *Georgia Straight*, are still around, but, as with fine wine, they are hard to come by. In many cases, the editors themselves have lost their copies in the course of transcontinental searching and various bad scenes.

O well. After the Solidarity Day march, which featured speakers like Gene McCarthy and (yes) Hubert Humphrey, while barring Carmichael and Tijerina from the platform, we all drank some beer, smoked some dope, and went to see *The Graduate*, a popular film of that era which featured some supertechnicolor footage of California which made us even more anxious to get out of town. Which we did in Wayne's failing black VW, Adolph, and after a short stay in New York, I went up to Vermont and signed papers giving us that legendary farm.

Back to Washington then to engineer moving the national office to the Big Apple. A big rental van had been brought down from New York by the people there, who had also rented a basement office on Claremont Avenue opposite Grant's Tomb to replace the one room on Broadway. Once the lease had been signed it was too late to think twice, but the new office put off even worse vibes than Washington could, if such a thing were possible. It had no sunlight at all and concrete walls which gave it a cavelike dampness and almost a penitentiary atmosphere. Following the New York City custom, such windows as there were had bars across them. And, although LNS was in theory moving in order to *expand*, the new quarters were a good deal smaller than the familiar Thomas Circle ones, necessitating partitioned offices the size of inadequate closets. I knew I'd have to spend some weeks there tying up LNS's loose ends and waiting for Verandah to tire of California and come home before I could even visit my new home in Vermont, so I set about moving from Washington with the distinct and surprising sensation that I was jumping from the cellblock into the dungeon. It was then early July and the heat in both cities was enough to curb anybody's good cheer.

We had accumulated quite an arsenal of equipment, files, and personal belongings in our Washington days. Loading the truck and several cars took all of one day and well into the night. As with the California departure, many details got left unattended, and many valuable papers and objects got stuffed into crates and envelopes, to be redis-covered weeks or months later, generally after they had lost their time value. The phones and Telex never got properly disconnected, the "Washington bureau" was left under vague controls (Michele, Marc Sommer, and a professional free-lance writer named Tom DeBaggio, whose minimum salary demands were far beyond our resources), and the lease on Thomas Circle was unwisely left to the *Free Press* to pay off. Most of my personal files, phonograph records, and furniture had been destroyed in a flood (broken water main) at Church Street, and were abandoned, along with my mahogany desk, by then thoroughly infested with every kind of crawling insect. I found myself sitting on the stoop at Church Street with Michele, who was sorry of the whole business; Peter Simon, whose stereo set had just then been stolen from his car; and several others. Though there was no reason to be, I was nostalgic.

There was something politically significant about that last tearful moment. And that was that the movement as we knew it had changed from flowers and yellow subma-rines, peace and brotherhood, to sober revolutionary com-mittees, Ché-inspired berets, even guns, and there was nothing we could do to stop it. We made the mistake of declaring LNS an organ of The Movement, and now that The Movement was sour and bitter, LNS had to follow. The house on Church Street was always open, even in the worst of times, to most anybody who needed it—Mrs. Lawrence, high-school runaways, people passing through, General Hershey Bar from Hollywood, chicks who came down from college to get one of Nathan Rappaport's fa-mous abortions, demonstrators, guys sleeping off a bad trip. We'd paid dearly for living in such a hostel, but we never seriously considered our "internal security" or stuff like that. Where we were headed there was no communal home, and no room for cats and dogs and children. The office on Thomas Circle was a good place to hang out as well as work, a place to smoke dope and sleep on the floor and play records, where there were no bosses or authority-chain and you could sunbathe on the roof. Where we were headed there were double locks on the door, special offices for "editors" and "business manager," pigeonholes for your mail, a receptionist's desk, and no windows. Most of us in Washington didn't really believe in "the revolution" to come, or else we acted like the revolution was right then and there; we tried to enjoy life as much as possible, took acid trips, went to the movies, and supported people because they were fun or well intentioned or in need. Where we were headed, most everybody believed fervently in "the revolution," and was working *toward* it—a revolution based on Marx and Lenin and Cuba and SDS and "the struggle"; and people were supported only on the basis of what they were *worth* to the revolution; and most of the things in life which were purely enjoyable were bourgeois comforts irrelevant to the news service, although not absolutely barred. In Washington we enjoyed printing recipes for psilocybin, articles about dried beef which fell from the sky, poetry about nature; we even sent out scores of paisley five-foot-long paper fishes and articles printed on blinding magenta paper. Where we were headed, LNS material was to be judged on its political relevance, true revolutionary sincerity, analytical Korrectness, even its consistency with "our ideological viewpoint."

Yet we couldn't stop this any more than the Fort Hill family could stop takeover of *AVATAR*, the true fathers of Haight-Ashbury prevent the pushers and pimps and exploiters from crowding in on the Summer of Love, or, for that matter, Dr. King prevent his nonviolent movement from turning to guns in the night. For me, as a pacifist, there was no alternative but to abandon what was becoming a zealous, disciplined, "militant" cadre of angry young journalists—"artists" no longer. (Even the terminology is quite telling; for while it is now considered very good to be "militant," I could never associate "militancy" with anything but the character disorder I stand *opposed* to.)

Once the truck was loaded and began its laborious journey out of town, it promptly broke down. Peter Cawley, a strapping youth who'd been working in the New York office for a few weeks, climbed out from behind the driver's seat and lit a cigarette on the curbstone. It was dawn. A pair of young black men approached us. "Hold on," Peter said with complete assurance, "we're gonna get hit." As the street guys came up, Peter stood up, unbuttoning his shirt and baring his massive chest. They just wanted a cigarette. "Sure, sure, here's a cigarette." I was dumbfounded at the way these New York slickers know the ropes, and duly impressed—though I couldn't see myself staring down two hostile characters on a deserted street at dawn. And I worried that such a jungle-trained attitude must come out of living in a jungle. Peter Cawley thus became for me the symbol of our New York office, physically strong, cynical, and defensive, but with a heart of gold. I was wrong, of course, because it turns out New Yorkers are by and large a pack of weaklings whose apparent cynicism is actually a much deeper loss of sensitivity to the whole world around them. If you don't believe that practically everybody in Manhattan is clinically mad, try looking at the faces on any subway car any time of day; a hopeless lot.

We arrived at Claremont Avenue many hours later and began unloading our stuff into corridors too narrow and doorways too crowded. Fortunately for me, I was still on good enough terms with a middle-class family in the Bronx to be allowed to store my personal belongings up there—bicycle, bed, and books. There was still the question of where I was to sleep, for all the Washington people were now refugees and we were forced to split up and beg floor space and couches from whichever friends were most beholden. I took to the lower East Side, living on alternate nights with Marty Jezer's cats and roaches, then with John Wilton and Brian Keating in the *AVATAR* loft, a big room housing four or five adults, two children, and pets. Clever Marshall told some old lady that he was a graduate student out of Kenyon College and got her West 76th Street apartment for three months, rent free, in exchange for feeding her expensive cat; and into this midtown palace moved Lazarus Quan and Sluggo Wasserman, who'd suddenly reappeared. I don't know where Allen Young went, but very shortly thereafter he left for Bulgaria and some kind of international youth conference which stressed revolutionary purism and kicked out "unwashed hippies." Craig Spratt floated around with no place to lay his head, as usual, and Sheila Ryan, who at the last minute had left the *Free Press* to join our northbound odyssey, moved in with George Cavalletto just down the street from the new office. In the arcane world of New Babylon, the lower East Side and upper West Side may as well be thousands of miles apart for the difference in the lives of their citizenry, so I honestly felt that our household had been ripped asunder by some awful political shake-up which we, simple folk, didn't quite understand.

Verandah had been gone two months now and all I knew of her life was a few fragmented telephone calls from Carmel and a poem I got in the mail. She'd apparently left Christopher (who later turned up on *CBS News* as a convicted dope dealer sentenced to twenty years in the state of Washington) and gone up to Oregon with a new young man, C. Michael Gies, son of the legendary Parker Gies, farmer and lawyer of Salem, Rain Country. Michael later came East with V and Laurie Dodge and Richard Wizansky, a poet from South Boston, and we all got properly mugged together less than an hour after their arrival in New York. Here's the poem:

WHEN IN THE COURSE OF HUMAN EVENTS

When in the course of human events,
it's a good day, Ray.
Though cars collide like warring dinosaurs,
the fourth of July
on the lower East side
must be swell.

So far, so long
in the Northwest wilderness,
I lie in my traitor's bed
from the boom,
for the fireworks have belched
an avalanche of eagles
to swoop me away
from my dreams
of your chinny-chin-chin
and your old soft shoe.

Spell it again!
It's a good day, Ray.
Where the eagles bit
my sides are torn
like ruffles from a petticoat.
Only your jack-be-nimble
stitch-in-time
can fasten back
my glory to the flag.

Carry me back from the Northwest wilderness
and into your lair,
for every boyscout needs a brownie,
a sadder but wiser
I'm still your girl.
Fiddle me back to your half-cocked hat,
then after a pause for a candy bar,
we'll pay the piper for the feast,
and shuffle off from Buffalo to Mars.

Peter Simon had a house in New York, though, and on one Monday we went to Jones Beach, and that was fun.

✻   ✻   ✻

We started a daily routine down on Claremont Avenue, a joyless attention to the details necessary to keep the news service alive. Much of my time was spent with John

Wilton and Wayne Hansen printing *AVATAR*, burning the
plates for same, buying paper and supplies with question-
able checks, and driving all the stuff around in Peter Cawley's VW Fun Bus. We took to smoking grass in Van Cort-
landt Park on upper Broadway, a nice place to feed your
head, and I introduced John to Dr. Brown's Cel-Ray Soda
at a local delicatessen. While all this was going on, though,
a curious tension had gripped the entire office, the first obvious result of which was that fewer and fewer news stories
were being written. All the nose-for-news Columbia drop-
outs who had been filing mountains of copy were now, it
seemed, hanging around the office and conversing in
hushed tones in corner-groups. Meetings were scheduled at
George's apartment with attendance limited to certain par-
tisans. People were always being pulled aside and whispered to. And the crux of the whole dilemma, the issue, it
was clear, was Marshall Bloom and what to *do* about him.

Marshall apparently intimidated the New York people, as well he might. He was the big man from Washington who had always handled LNS as a personal cause, who
was in charge of finances, and who, with me, Sluggo, and
Marc Sommer, owned the corporation which published the
news service. Since Sluggo and Marc were not viewed as
permanent New York workers, and I was supposed to be
splitting for Vermont one of those days, Marshall was the
last vestige of the old order, which the New York folk
found reprehensible and irresponsible. It finally became
clear that if George et al. were to run the news service their
way, Marshall would have to go—but that was like kicking
Mickey Mantle off the Yankees. It was unfair, inhumane,
and ruthless, but a purge was going on.

When Marshall was around the office, people
snapped at him, shouted at him. When would he give up
the LNS checking accounts and turn over the financial
powers to the new business manager? When would he turn
over the corporation to a committee of *all* the people who
worked for LNS? (These people included many who'd literally just arrived, some from the New York environs and a

few from as far away as Chicago.) The analogy was repeatedly voiced that SDS had been founded by a bunch of "social democrats" (very bad) but ultimately turned over to
"real revolutionaries"; Bloom and I were the "social democrats" in this instance. When Marshall was *not* around the
office, which grew to be most of the time, he was accused
of far worse things than mere freakiness. Kids who'd never
even met him would approach me with questions like Is it
true Marshall Bloom is a thief? sex pervert? compulsive
liar?

Well, William Alfred, who is a very good poet, once
wrote that we human creatures are like skunks—"we stink
when we're afraid or hurt." Marshall had power over LNS,
as well as a formidable arsenal of friendships, contacts, and
psychic powers of his own, and the new order at LNS had
to demolish him in order to get the power. And they had to
get the power, or thought they did, because they wanted to
do a news service substantially *different* from the one Marshall had created, a news service which would be more serious, more militant, more straight, edited and managed by
a collective and not an individual. They were afraid of
Marshall's horning in on their vision of LNS, and hurt by
his personal greatness. Our position, of course, was that
they should go start their *own* goddamn news service if
they wanted one so badly, but power struggles never work
like that, for neither side wants the insecurity of starting
from nothing, no reputation or history (though that's how
we started). And it was also true that the "market" out
there couldn't adequately support one radical news service,
let alone two. So all kinds of stuff was going on—sheets of
paper signed by scores of people I'd never heard of, purporting to be the new, legal Board of Directors of LNS;
forty-eight-hour-long meetings at which nothing was decided and "unauthorized persons" were physically ejected;
and finally a complete polarization between two groups,
the Vulgar Marxists (all New York people except Allen
Young) and the Virtuous Caucus (all Washington people
except Steve Diamond).

Alas, I can't make this whole scene sound funny or even *ironic* because it was so ugly in itself; nor can I fill you, dear reader, too full of observations about how *symptomatic* all this was of the state of the movement. But I'm searching for a way to say that I don't condemn the Vulgar Marxists (my title). I don't even think they are *bad* people, or that they acted in any way that isn't absolutely typical of the human race and particularly of politicians. But their politics was communal socialism, whereas ours was something like anarchism; and while we could cheerfully keep a few socialists around, they couldn't function as they planned with even one anarchist in the house, one Marshall Bloom, who would go out in the afternoon and buy a glorious collator, or take an unexpected trip. Their method of running the news service was the Meeting and the Vote, ours was Magic. We lived on Magic, and still do, and I have to say it beats anything *systematic*.

Anyway, I'm laying groundwork here for the next chapter, in which the angry words and hostile glares between the Vulgar Marxists and the Virtuous Caucus turn into high adventure and bloody thrills. It is important for you to know that both groups met in secret, night after night, and both devised lurid fantasies against the other, and both found the members of the other group to be base fellows. In short, our few weeks in New York virtually halted all the ongoing research and news gathering of the organization, and whipped one and all into a frenzy of protective fury and personal loyalty. Our caucus was hopelessly outnumbered, but it was made up of people who'd been through a lot of shit together already, and had already made numerous personal commitments to the news service; theirs was much larger in numbers, but a fairly recent coalition. And we had Magic (read: God) on our side.

In the middle of the whole fracas, Eldridge Cleaver came to town. His arrival had long been anticipated, for he was the guy who'd bring us all back together again, who was truly taking over the Bay Area in California, who was eloquent and tough and pure of heart. In a time when heroes were few and far between, he was kind of a last hope. Yet when he came everybody at LNS was somewhere else, and I found myself the only person in the office free to go downtown and interview him. This happened, in the course of things, because I was printing *AVATAR* with John Wilton instead of attending either of the caucus meetings then going on. So John, Craig, and I climbed into Supercar and sped downtown, ace reporters hot on the heels of the elusive Cleaver.

We met Lenox Raphael, a black reporter for the *East Village Other* (and author of *Ché!*) at the door to Cleaver's hotel suite, and luckily John knew Raphael from some previous scene so they had a good chat and we got into the hotel room with only a small amount of defensive self-proving. The front room was full of happy people, both black and white, drinking wine and obviously feeling on the brink of sure victory over life's terrible obstacles. And Eldridge Cleaver himself was in the bedroom answering phone calls and dictating into a small tape recorder. Bobby Seale, who is the chairman of the Black Panther Party, was there too but he was so tired he just smiled hello and fell asleep. That's the ultimate statement of trust and friendship, when somebody will fall asleep beside you. We sat at the foot of Cleaver's bed and rapped with him for an hour or more very quietly and with instinctive unspoken understandings flashing back and forth between our eyes. We talked a little about politics, the movement, and that kind of stuff, but also about more abstract (yet more real) concerns like love, beauty, the *quality* of life. Simply, we became *friends*. You know what I mean—or else I can't tell you.

One of the most impressive things about Eldridge was that, despite being shot up by the cops and all, he just didn't have the kind of *hard-line* mentality which would have been perfectly justified for a man in his position; to the contrary, his entire being bespoke wisdom and kindness. He told us to be wary of supporting everybody who called himself a revolutionary, that some of these revolu-

tionaries were, you know, sort of in the same place as cops
only from the other side of the issue. Yes we certainly knew
that already but hearing it from him made it seem all the
more truthful. We nodded our heads. We knew. We left
the hotel feeling just fine, skipping along the sidewalk, digging the sunshine—like you've just left your lover's bed,
and you'll see him/her again tomorrow, and you're not
hungry or tired or anything bad.

We buzzed on over to Marshall's pad on 76th,
where everybody was smoking hash and watching an old
movie on TV. Stevie Wonder had gotten over his undig-
nified departure from Washington and was back once again;
it was good to see him, it was like the extended family
being back together again, and we cooked up an inexpen-
sive candlelight dinner and talked about the holy Cleaver
and wondered how Verandah was doing in her desperate
efforts to escape Oregon. We put on our glad rags after taking hot showers at the expense of the cat lady who owned
the place. Thus refreshed, John and I returned to Claremont Avenue in the city-darkness to have another go at
printing *AVATAR*.

Uptown, the office was as quiet as when we'd left it
that afternoon, but Steve Diamond was hanging around in
the pressroom reading and digging the pages of *AVATAR*
that we had already printed. I immediately told him all
about the happy time with Eldridge Cleaver, told him
about the revolutionaries who are worse than cops and so
forth. That seemed to strike Steve Diamond pretty hard.
He began to speak of himself. He was confused and unhappy. As one of the first people in the New York office, he
was inclined to side with his familiar allies from Columbia,
but on the other hand he couldn't believe that Marshall
Bloom was as bad as his friends had described. Neutrality
was next to impossible. And he had the feeling that George
and George's right-hand man Dan McCauslin, a former reporter for *Women's Wear Daily,* would snuff him out when
the time came. He was uneasy about purges in general,
whether of M. Bloom or anyone else. He doubted he could

continue working for LNS if the superhostility vibes went on much longer. In short, he was looking for some Virtue left in the world, and there we were! Steve Diamond became a member of the Virtuous Caucus because he needed some sunlight and we were, at that moment, full of it. Let the chips fall where they may, he was with us. It's so nice to make a friend!

Last time I saw Steve Diamond, he was wearing my Sioux headband and grinning good-bye on his way to Big Sur.

One more thing. Steve Diamond, being himself something of a spaced-out operator, had persuaded the distributor of the Beatles' new movie, *Magical Mystery Tour,* that he could win goodwill for the film and have an opportunity to test its impact on U.S. audiences if he'd donate the first two American showings to Liberation News Service as a benefit. On August 11, then, the movie was to be unveiled at the Fillmore East, home base of the psychedelic generation, and Steve Diamond was in charge of all the arrangements, including the collection of box-office receipts—which were estimated to be $15,000. Given our intensifying destitution and debt over the last year, that money was absolutely essential to the continuation of the news service.

The stage was thus set for the guns of August.

*　　*　　*

"Friendship is evanescent in every man's experience, and remembered like heat lightning in past summers. Fair and flitting like a summer cloud;—there is always some vapor in the air, no matter how long the drought; there are even April showers. Surely from time to time, for its vestiges never depart, it floats through our atmosphere. It takes place, like vegetation in so many materials, because there is such a law, but always without permanent form, though ancient and familiar as the sun and moon, and as sure to come again. The heart is forever inexperienced. They silently gather as by magic, these never failing, never quite deceiving visions, like the bright and fleecy clouds in the calmest and clearest days. The Friend is some fair floating isle of palms eluding the mariner in Pacific seas. Many are the dangers to be encountered, equinoctial gales and coral reefs, ere he may sail before the constant trades. But who would not sail through mutiny and storm even over Atlantic waves, to reach the fabulous retreating shores of some continent man? . . .

"Who does not walk on the plain as amid the columns of Tadmore of the desert? There is on the earth no institution which Friendship has established; it is not taught by any religion; no scripture contains its maxims. It has no temple, not even a solitary column . . .

"However, our fates at least are social. Our courses do not diverge; but as the web of destiny is woven it is fulled, and we are cast more and more into the centre. Men naturally, though feebly, seek this alliance, and their actions faintly foretell it. We are inclined to lay the chief stress on likeness and not on difference.

"No word is oftener on the lips of men than Friendship, and indeed no thought is more familiar to their aspirations. All men are dreaming of it, and its drama, which is always a tragedy, is enacted daily. It is the secret of the universe. You may tread the town, you may wander the country, and none shall ever speak of it, yet thought is everywhere busy about it, and the idea of what is possible in this respect affects our behavior toward all new men and women and a great many old ones. Nevertheless, I can remember only two or three essays on this subject in all literature. No wonder that the Mythology, and Arabian Nights, and Shakespeare, and Scott's novels entertain us,—we are poets and fablers and dramatists and novelists ourselves. We are continually acting a part in a more interesting drama than any written. We are dreaming that our Friends are our *Friends,* and that we are our Friends' *Friends* . . .

"What is commonly honored with the name of Friendship is no very profound or powerful instinct. Men do not, after all, *love* their Friends greatly. I do not often see the farmers made seers and wise to the verge of insanity by their Friendship for one another. They are not often transfigured and translated by love in each other's presence. I do not observe them purified, refined, and elevated by the love of a man. If one abates a little the price of his wood, or gives a neighbor his vote at town-meeting, or a barrel of apples, or lends him his wagon frequently, it is esteemed a rare instance of Friendship. Nor do the farmers' wives lead lives consecrated to Friendship. I do not see the pair of farmer friends of either sex prepared to stand against the world. There are only two or three couples in history. To say that a man is your Friend, means commonly no more than this, that he is not your enemy. Most contemplate only what would be the accidental and trifling advantages of Friendship, as that the Friend can assist in time of need, by his substance, or his influence, or his counsel; but he who foresees such advantages in this relation proves himself blind to its real advantage, or indeed wholly inexperienced in the relation itself. Such services are particular and menial compared with the perpetual and all-embracing service which it is. Even the utmost good-will and harmony and practical kindness are not sufficient for Friendship, for Friends do not live in harmony merely, as some say, but in melody. We do not wish for Friends to feed and clothe our bodies,—neighbors are kind enough for that—but to do the like office to our spirits. For this few are rich enough, however well disposed they may be."

Henry David Thoreau, *A Week on the Concord and Merrimack Rivers*

CHAPTER NINE

The guns of August

I. The Heist

Well I have to admit now that the heist was my idea, and now that I think of it, the idea first came to me in the *AVATAR* loft. John Wilton and I had retired there one night after a lot of printing, and we started talking to Brian Keating. Brian was once the editor of *AVATAR* in Boston, later in New York, and he was the incredible Irish who'd heisted and destroyed 25,000 copies of an issue of *AVA-TAR* produced by the splinter group opposed to Fort Hill. They were talking about that one for months in Boston. Brian and I had in common a kind of chronic passion for dazzling schemes, Dadaistic tricks intended to "blow the minds" of the largest portion of the world we could reach. We both would have done well making Hollywood movies in the 1930s, I think, but alas, except for Kesey and that crowd on the Coast, there are just no merrie pranksters left. Anyway, I came up with the idea of the heist and John and Brian added bits and pieces to it and we shouted back and forth at each other new suggestions and innuendos until at last the sun was up and we'd spun a most fantastic plan to solve the ills of LNS and our family of friends. "The guns of August," Brian chuckled as he fell into sleep. Gulley John, who is three, called it something like "Bun Ogga."

Something *had* to be done, after all, for to leave bad enough alone meant simply that Marshall, Sluggo, Craig, Lazarus, and all the people who had made LNS what it was would be stripped of any role within the news service and just go looking for a whole new life. LNS would be a propaganda outlet for SDS, an option we had long ago rejected as unfit. The Vulgar Marxists had im-

163

ported a sizable group of people to help them run the news service, and we couldn't expect our little band to long survive in an atmosphere of hostility and rejection not only from the cops and the government but also from their coworkers. We had a legal recourse in that we owned the corporate papers and the name Liberation News Service but that wasn't going to stop the New York crowd from publishing under the same imprint, and the whole idea of suing them through an expensive and time-consuming court process was repugnant to us. Clearly, then, the only solution was to move the news service—press, collator, files, typewriters, and all—out of New York to some place, any place, where we could be ourselves again, and where George Cavalletto didn't own the lease on the building. It was necessary to do this when none of the New York folk were around, in order to avoid physical violence and a literal "power" struggle which we'd surely lose. I kept thinking of Peter Cawley's broad chest. And it was necessary to find some money to rent new quarters in another place and finance moving costs. Most important, it was essential that we keep the whole scheme under tighter wraps than we'd ever managed in the past; one leak, and we were through.

Steve Diamond was the key man, for as a member of the original New York group, he would know their habits well enough to chart a sound Heist plan; he was the double-agent, the Insider, which every good job requires. He was also the Beatles man and had access to $15,000 in LNS box-office receipts, including many checks which we could quite legally cash. Thus the scenario was perfect: Steve Diamond would lead his New York cronies on to trusting him thoroughly to handle the money, and while the entire New York group was blissfully watching the Beatles movie at the Fillmore East, the entire Washington group would be on the other side of New York lifting everything in the office that wasn't nailed down! Steve would channel the advance ticket money into our hands at once so we could get another place, and he'd take the door money with him when he left the theater that night. It was a tight schedule, and it depended on the assumption that nobody from the New York group would matter-of-factly decide to work that night, but we thought we could pull it off. Things being as they were, we were ready to try.

The first problem was Steve Diamond himself, and could we *trust* him not to betray us? (You can imagine, dear reader, just how uptight people can get when they are planning burn schemes involving sums of money and materials. All at once, everybody is suspect. Humanity as a whole is divided into those who are *with you* all the way, and everybody else. This kind of thinking is common to all capitalistic corporations, socialist states, governments, publishing empires, and power groups, and to not a few simple households, genetic families, bowling leagues, and bridge clubs. I'm not saying it's good or bad, just that it's probably happened to you in your lifetime and will happen again. Confess.) I thought we could trust him because I could see no motive he might have for playing along with us; but I *knew* we could trust him because I'd made his friendship. The problem was also resolved for the others over a short period of time, perhaps a week, and thereafter everybody took Steve's allegiance for granted and for good.

The second problem was where to move. Both Steve and I thought Boston was the perfect place, Washington being too hot (in several senses) and California too far. But Marshall insisted on a farm, said it was high time to abandon the urban nightmare anyway, and who knows when we'd have the money to buy a farm *again*. So the heist, which was to culminate a squabble over personalities and also over ideology, was to take on the added dimension of an urban-rural rift. The morning after the scheme was hatched, Marshall and Steve took $5000 of the advance benefit money and went north to Massachusetts looking for farmland, which they eventually found in Montague. Steve was angry with Marshall for being so uncompromising, but gave up his vision of Boston with its many young people, universities, and added Head-type attractions, once he cast eyes on the green hills of western Massachusetts. The farm they bought was in the shadow of its own protective mountain, rolling and open (sixty acres), with a seventeen-room red house and an enormous barn rich in grain and character. "I never spoke with God,/Nor visited in Heaven,/Yet certain am I of the spot/As if the chart were given." Emily Dickinson said that.

Everything about the heist, seen through our eyes at that time, was perfect. It added insult to injury; the whole crowd of "them" would sit through the Beatles movie, fairly reveling in the full-houses and counting all their hula-dollars before they were heisted. It was to be the ultimate defeat for Allen Young; he'd be in *Bulgaria* at some kind of *conference* when the roof fell on him! (We could even envision the telegram he'd receive there: CRISIS. BLOOM BAND TOOK THE GOODS. COME HOME.) It got all the members of the Virtuous Caucus out of New Babylon and into Edenlike green pastures, leaving the Vulgar Marxists to the grime and ca-ca they so enjoyed. It was crazy, harebrained, funny, challenging, and heavy—in short in the best tradition of Church Street and Thomas Circle.

And just when we thought we had it made, when the challenge was dimming and the excitement telescoping down, Marshall added a wrinkle which would make the whole job ever more difficult and heroic: only criminals move furniture in the dark, he said, there's something very sneaky about that, so we should do the whole thing in *broad daylight.* Gasp. Broad *what?* When? What about George, who lived half a block away from the office on Claremont? They'd be *working* in daylight! Not on Sunday, he returned. Sunday night the film was to be shown, so on Sunday *morning* we'd pull off the heist; for, you see, the Vulgar Marxists, entirely unlike the raggedy crew in Washington, never worked on Sunday, and only occasionally on Saturday. And, since they would have all been up late Saturday night, they'd of course sleep till noon on Sunday.

Moreover, we could heist the news service at 10:00 A.M., which was when the building superintendent *always* took his kids to Jones Beach, and our archenemies wouldn't even discover it till Monday morning, when they dragassed in for another week of "work." O it was delicious and sinister. The only hitch was that Steve Diamond would be left in New York to pick up the box-office money that night and if by quirk of fate the deed was discovered before the movie started, there'd be hell to pay for Steve—who would probably lose the money as well. But quirks of fate, though they may rule *our* lives, have nothing to do with Vulgar Marxists, right?

❀   ❀   ❀

Details, details. Marshall went down to the post office and registered a change of address for LNS, so that all our mail would be sped north before it even brushed Claremont Avenue, opposite Grant's Tomb. The writers and typists and printers went to work on an LNS mailing to be sent from the farm the morning after the heist, explaining our sudden decision and our internecine dispute. The envelopes for said mailing had to be addressographed in advance, since all the addressograph plates would doubtless get packed at the bottom of a large crate, and these plates were worth more than the press itself, they were irreplaceable, they were the only existing record of LNS's fat mailing list. The first issue from the farm would be, by chance or magic, issue Number 100.

❀   ❀   ❀

In the middle of everything, Verandah came back from Oregon with Laurie, Richard, and Michael. She had made it on Marshall's last hundred dollars, which was a secret between the two of them. She'd been picking strawberries—good practice for Vermont—on some large Oregon farm in an attempt, hopeless, to raise enough for the trip East. I told her all the hair-raising stories of late, concluding with the great attempt to oust Marshall and the complex scheme to heist the presses, have fun, and get LNS a farm, all in a swoop. She fairly gurgled with delight at this last bit, and got right into the spirit of things. Now we were an extended-family back together again, and prepared to stand against the movement or the world. We all loved each other intensely, and told each other so. Our friends from Washington, including the saintly Bill Higgs, drifted up to the Big Apple as H-Day approached. All kinds of O K people, including some underground editors who subscribed to LNS, were prepared to stand by us in this latest assault on the forces of constipation. We felt invincible.

We decided to celebrate by having a beer at the neighborhood restaurant-bar around the corner from the Claremont Avenue office, so we went over there and had a glorious time. But the local Puerto Ricans took what I have since decided was justifiable offense at my Indian shirt (which they called a "dress") and as we left the restaurant-bar, John Wilton and I found ourselves flat strung out on the pavement and Verandah was talking to the Puerto Ricans in mixed Spanish explaining we came in friendship and all that kind of stuff. John went down first with a right to the chin. I knew I was next and actually it didn't hurt till afterwards, when it hurt a lot. I just floated through the air and onto the pretty cobblestones of 122nd Street, thinking to myself "This is the way the world ends." It seemed unfair, though, that my family always got hurt when it wasn't trying to offend anybody, yet somehow always escaped any injury when trying its best to infuriate somebody or everybody.

Well the plot was doing very nicely, Steve salting away the Beatles money in a little Polish bank on the lower East Side, and everybody else figuring out the logistics of the move, so V and I and our new farm family went north to Vermont and tackled a whole new set of problems there. We didn't expect to come back and actually participate in the heist, since there were enough people to do the physical labor already; we planned to be on the receiving end, in

Montague, when the victorious Bloom's Band arrived with
the loot. But of course it happened elsewise; Marshall
called our neighbors in Vermont on Saturday, August 10,
and said our good vibes were essential to the success of the
project. We never argue with logic like that, so Verandah,
Wayne Hansen, Ellen Snyder, and I left the little farmhouse in the dead of night and arrived in New York at 3:00
A.M. Sunday, or zero hour minus seven. We were singing
relevant contemporary ditties like

> Late last night, when they were all in bed,
> The Virtuous Caucus stole the presses from the shed,
> And when they woke up this morning,
> They all freaked out and said:
> "There was a hot time in the old town last night."

and

> No Big Apple, no Big Apple,
> No Big Apple over meeeeeeeee!
> And before I'll be a slave, I'll be buried in my grave,
> And go home to Mon'gue and be freeeee!

Dawn shortly came and, one by one, the conspirators
slipped away from Marshall's pad and headed on up to the
million-dollar bash. When I got there at 9:00 A.M., the
office was completely cleared, press and collator waiting on
wooden dollies, dozens of cardboard boxes with our lives
stuffed into them, all crowded against the front door like
barricades against a sudden bust. A huge rented truck with
hydraulic lift was parked two blocks away, waiting for the
superintendent's carful of beach-happy children to pass by.
(Are you *sure* he goes to Jones Beach *every* Sunday?) The
office was crowded with whispering, nervous people
crouched on the floors and on all the chairs, listening to the
suddenly ear-shattering noises of New York on a Sunday
morning and waiting for time to pass.

*   *   *

I find myself embarrassed at telling the story. Perhaps it's because I'm telling it as I would have told it then, recalling how my mind worked in those troubled hours, all the conceit and hostility and resentment and uptightness. I feel very different now. It is as if many thousands of years have passed since these events occurred, I have seen such things and been such places and experienced such a succession of changes. Perhaps my memory is affected, and I remember these things as worse than they seemed at the time. "Generations have trod, have trod, have trod." Wars are made of small conceits indeed. And how infinitely petty our world can be when we can't see *through* it! I mean no insult to any of the people herein described, but that we were possessed of dark spirits in those days. Some of us, alas, remain so, but many others have freed themselves. The dread presence may, however, return at any moment. I am speaking to you from beyond the world right now. Please tell my loved ones I am well and happy on the other side. Greet them for me and tell them we will be together again here, in the by-and-by.

*   *   *

Steve Diamond motioned me over to his apartment next door. He had a green strongbox with $6,000 inside. This was placed in a bowler hat which I wore on my head. I strolled down the avenue in a Chaplin parody and sat behind the wheel of Nellybelle waiting for the dam to break.

*   *   *

At 10:15 A.M., the superintendent had finished packing his car, and he took off down the street for Jones Beach. A moment later, he rounded the block and went back to his apartment for some forgotten item, maybe suntan lotion or a towel. Activity in the office, which had just burst, froze scared. He climbed back into his car and left for the beach a second time. We waited for his return.

When five minutes had passed without further evidence of the super, the door to the office burst open as the big truck lumbered up to the curb. Bill Lewis, the former editor of *OFF* in Nashville, was behind the wheel and Stevie Marsden from New College in Florida was his helpmate. An enormous racket was starting as heavy equipment and a monstrous assortment of furniture and boxes was hauled up basement stairs to the sidewalk. The neighbors hung out their windows asking questions like "You guys moving?" (They were clearly not upset by the thought of losing us.) Columbia's International students, who dormed across the street, stared from their cubicles. Passing policemen took casual note of the operation. Strolling tourists examined us carefully. Motorists stopped to check it out. Small children taunted us. Everybody on the block found the whole scene vastly entertaining and interesting—except the sleeping George Cavalletto and his roommates up the block.

Steve Lerner, writing in the *Village Voice*, called it a "daring daylight raid on (our) own offices." Somebody in Collegiate Press Service said it was "the most bizarre story out of the underground since Valerie shot Andy." For two hours, hundreds of blasé New Yorkers watched a great heist taking place; we could have taken the contents of the superintendent's apartment as well without causing much of a stir. It wasn't theft in legal terms, but it was an extraordinarily frantic moving-party. When the office had been stripped of everything except essentially worthless or personal items, the door was closed and locked on it. The end of New York City. The truck was full to overflowing and some items were crammed into the automobiles nearby, which formed a northbound caravan. By noon the sidewalk was empty and the neighborhood deathly quiet. Nothing seemed changed from the outside, and nothing was to be discovered all that day and well into the next. I pulled out last with the money under my hat and sand in my eyes.

We stopped for breakfast at a small town in Connecticut. The management of the diner was reluctant to be our host, but we persevered and finally got eggs, orange juice, and coffee for $1.25 apiece. I sat next to the $6,000 and wondered who am I? What is happening here? What will be the end of this adventure? We were still numb from the tension at the scene-of-the-crime, and slightly incredulous at the ease with which we had pulled off the stunt. All of the movement would be shocked when the story broke, for this was the most spectacular case of intergroup warfare since the CIO expelled its commies. Underground newspapers would take a cue from this, as papers got heisted here and there, and one faction ousted the other. The national news media, never slow to undermine counterestablishment efforts, would take a consuming interest in this incident.

And could the New York group take this sitting down? I wondered for the first time. Could anybody be made to appear so foolish, be victims of such thorough subversion and espionage, be robbed of everything they considered their own right under their noses, and not panic and strike back with irrational and bloodthirsty fury? Now the trip was half-done, didn't there remain a dark side yet to descend? These questions and more flooded my mind as I drove the Merritt Parkway, on which all the bridges are unique in design and construction, to New Haven, then up through Hartford and Springfield and into the north country.

At the farm in Montague, all was quiet. Those who had arrived before us were sitting on the lawn taking in sunshine. The truck took a circuitous route, and hence arrived later. The rooms of the house were mostly bare, just a mattress here and there, a few candles, some unpacked boxes, and a couple of chairs, plus that old nemesis, Fiendbox, ruthless, intrusive Telephone. Curse my luck for participating in an incarnation when the Telephone was in vogue, and the Big Bummer had its electronic tentacle stretched into nearly everybody's home comfort. Not, anymore, mine.

The truck arrived to much cheering and general celebration. The heist was now a fact, the goods were delivered. I handed the $6,000 over to Cathy Hutchison, Steve Diamond's girlfriend, to be deposited first thing Monday morning in an Amherst, Mass., bank. After good words were exchanged all round, the press was sent on to a neighbor's barn for storage, as insurance against the possibility of a raid by the Yorkers. This, it was agreed, was a remote likelihood considering the distance between Montague and New York and the relatively more effective reprisals the left-behinds could take—publicity and propaganda campaigns, most probably. They *would* have to strike back.

Down in New York, it was a normal summer day. Dogs bit men, the sun bore down mercilessly, the entire population got charged so many dollars each for the right to go on living. George Cavalletto, Sheila Ryan, Miriam Bokser, Dan McCauslin, and the rest of the local LNS talent stayed home, presumably reading the *Times* and thinking about that night's big benefit on Second Avenue. Nobody went near the Claremont office, and none of the neighbors bothered to inform the building superintendent of the bustling moving scene which had taken place. Steve Diamond was next door, at Number 150, getting ready to vacate his apartment without notice to the landlord. By nightfall, some six thousand New Yorkers had gathered at the Fillmore East theater, where they apparently enjoyed watching films by Newsreel and *Magical Mystery Tour* by the Beatles. A few churlish letters complaining of the noise and delays in the theater appeared in the following week's *Village Voice*, but hell you can't please everybody. So calm was the evening that Steve Diamond decided to go back to his apartment and sleep rather than set out for Massachusetts in the middle of the night.

In the middle of the night that was the first night for a dozen people in a big red house in the unlikely town of Montague, Massachusetts, not much happened. It got darker than those people could remember darkness ever being, and more still than they could recall the world ever sounding. Gone now were the streetlamps, motors, jars of marijuana; now was the peace beyond the war. As I am writing, it is a year to the day of that night, and the stillness and darkness remain unbroken. There was a touch of autumn in the air, a chill which August often brings in the mountains, but there was no fire yet in the big wood stove.

Morning came. No cock crowed in Montague, those people had no animals yet. But in New York, Monday started, Monday with its rumblings and subways and speed, awful Monday that the whole world faced up to with a special distaste, the day when "the business of America" resumed after its brief lull. Steve Diamond got a telephone call quite early that morning from a friend not associated with LNS, asking did he know that the office had been completely heisted, probably by Bloom's Band? No, he didn't know that. Hadn't he better go over there and see if the rumor was true and call back to verify it if it was? Sure thing, he would do that. And, sure enough, the office was bare of everything except frantic people calling up other people in attempts to discover exactly where the freaks had taken the press. Nobody had even guessed at a farm in Massachusetts, there was no reason to think of anything so far-out. Steve Diamond professed great shock at this foul deed and left the city as fast as he could.

Comes the telling flaw, the quirk of fate. The New York faction dispatched someone to the post office, rightly guessing that they might find the whereabouts of the press through the forwarding address Bloom was surely clever enough to have left. The post office gave them much more than that; the post office gave them the entire LNS mailing Number 99, which it refused to send via second-class mail because a group called The Motherfuckers had charged into the LNS office two nights before and themselves stuffed mailing Number 99 with a broadsheet—called a "third-class enclosure" by the U.S. mails. Thus they knew that the goods were in Montague, Massachusetts (where's that?), and had the world's *second* copy of the LNS mailing list placed in their laps. They called Marshall's telephone in Montague (wise man see that telephone places him at enemy's disposal) and railed at him, but Marshall said stuff like come on up here and we'll talk it over, convinced that the beauty of the farm and its potential value to the news service would win at least some of them over, and this necessary wound would be healed.

Instead, a posse was being gathered. A black rock group, The Children of God, was recruited along with sundry friends and neighbors of the Yorkers from the lower East Side. Four or so autos, including Peter Cawley's famous Fun Bus, were gathered together, and when they left for Montague, approximately thirty white-hot people, some of whom had actually worked for LNS, were in them. They got out of New York at about 8:00 P.M., and as midnight neared found themselves in Montague.

As midnight neared, I found myself in Montague with five of my Vermont family alongside—two of whom, Ellen and Verandah, had participated in the heist. Being up in Vermont without a phone, we didn't anticipate meeting our New York allies at all; we had simply yielded to an irresistible impulse Monday night to bring warm bread and salt down to Montague and thus cheer up our friends there. Our own household was barely a month old, but it seemed like Green Mountain granite compared to the furnitureless settlement down in Massachusetts. But midnight was nearing, and we thought it high time to begin the hour-long trip home. So, after good-evenings to all, we went out to our car and turned over the motor.

II. The Raid

Before Michael could back out of the driveway, we were surrounded. Peter Cawley politely, but firmly, asked for the keys to the ignition. Michael, innocent of the whole dispute, was perplexed. Meanwhile, Norman Jenks, one of George's roommates, was under the hood yanking out the distributor cap from the VW engine. Lights flashed everywhere as car after car pulled into the farm driveway. Each of the invaders was carrying something—sticks, mostly, though one had a knife and a beanbrained fellow named Tom (later expelled by the Yorkers from their midst) was waving a metal rod wildly in the air. Very few words needed to be said, it was absolutely evident that we were hostages now. One by one, we left the car and were marched by our captors into the farmhouse through the back door. Don't try to escape, we were told, or you'll get hurt. There were suddenly five of us sitting on the bare floor of the back bedroom, surrounded by twice that number of armed Marxists. Through the open bedroom door, I could see Marshall, wearing shorts, being enveloped by waves of people coming through the front door.

Their first question was "Where's the press?" The press was worth $4,000 when brand-new, considerably less after any use at all, and even less than that after five thousand *AVATARs* and two long, unprofessional moving jobs in a little more than a month; but it was an emotional symbol, even an icon, for LNS I suppose. Personally, I would not have wanted it around my home. But the question "Where's the press?" was asked a half-dozen times in succession, each time to no answer at all from Marshall. All I knew of it was that the press was somewhere else in Montague, at some neighbor's barn, the location and name of the family never having been offered me. But when Marshall declined to provide the answer, various members of the raiding party asked me, and everybody else in the jail, where the press was, and of course didn't believe our earnest professions of ignorance. I applaud Marshall's courage in holding his ground, but I could see the situation getting very dangerous and, had I known, I certainly would have told them where that goddamn press was.

Meanwhile, a thorough search-and-destroy mission was sweeping the house and barn. Somebody whom I did not recognize was dismantling the telephone (well, I can't blame him). Chairs were overturned, furniture smashed, windows kicked in by zealous boots, items and artifacts and legal papers scooped up and brought to George and Peter, who were as much in charge of the operation as anyone. Bill Lewis's vial of pills was crushed and kicked away, and all the cars disabled. Some of our lady friends had begun to scream and cry, especially when the errant Tom decided he was a Nazi and took to beating them over the heads with his metal rod. The deed to the farm, some LNS checks, ownership papers for the corporation were found and turned over to George, who prized them in spite of the obvious fact that they were in themselves worthless. The press, the press, the press was still missing, as was the profit from the Beatles movie.

My mind raced as I saw the squad assigned to interrogating Marshall get progressively more angry. Surely, I thought, the incredible racket being made in this house will reach the neighbors, who will call the police—for the farm had reasonably close neighbors and the police, for the first time in my life, were the only people who could *save* us. It didn't even occur to me that night that there was some real irony in my praying for the *police* to come and end this nightmare. The other salvation, I remembered, lay in Bill Lewis and Steve Marsden, who were not at the farm but out in Montague somewhere in the big rented truck; when they pulled up, I hoped, they would see without much trouble that the house was being destroyed and its people held by force, and they would continue on in their truck and get the police. The whole police syndrome was working full-time in the minds of our captors, too, for they often spoke with trepidation about getting this job done before the police showed up, and repeatedly advised me not to make a break for it in order to reach the police. We were thus an all-American group, hung up on authority and violence—the side in the legal right hoping for rescue by the cops, and the other side, having no legal ground to stand on, assuming the role of cops themselves. Jailing, searching, destroying, beating.

Now the Marshall squad announced it was getting down to business—just give us the press and the money now and get it over with, no more bullshit, they said. Just like a tree standing by the water, Bloom would not be moved. Three or four guys began to belt him across the face, in the stomach, in the groin, while the rest of us watched from our little cell. Now Marshall was bleeding, scarlet rivers running down from his face across his chest and down his legs. Now Marshall was naked and limp. Now his body itself was being tossed, banged against a wall, kicked to the floor. And then he, and his tormentors, disappeared from our vision.

"You're going to kill him, you're going to kill him!" cried Cathy Hutchison, now hysterical with grief and fear. She spoke for all of us. "Yes, we will kill him, and not just him, if we don't get what we came for," a grinning youth—also unknown to me—said. And monstrous noises came from the next room—thuds and cracking belts and groans—while we were warned to give up the press and the money before our pal was cold dead. It was an old police and gangster trick, actually rooted in Romantic mythology (the same scene as ours appears, for example, in *Tosca*)—awful torments are inflicted on one person in an adjoining room while another person, who loves the victim, is pumped for information or loot. We couldn't tell whether the noises from the living room were legitimate homicide or a staged melodrama of flying furniture and the like, but from what we had just witnessed, we couldn't risk it. Cathy offered a $6,000 cashier's check made out to her—the green strongbox in the bowler hat—in exchange for Marshall's life. (It was a bargain.) She signed the check over to Liberation News Service (liberation!) and handed it to a smug George Cavalletto. With the check and the deed to the farm (which George actually seemed to believe was negotiable for the $5,000 placed in down-payment), the entire Beatles profit seemed to be in the hands of the raiders, and only the press remained at large. Mercifully, the noises subsided, and a thoroughly beaten Marshall emerged from the other room and slumped against the wall with us.

A few minutes before the raid began, as I was leaving the farmhouse for Vermont, Marshall had said that if they used violence against any of the people in the house, their case before The Movement, underground editors, and the public would be destroyed. They would not use violence, he had predicted, because use of violence would prove beyond a doubt our contention that this crowd was moved by hatred and despair, not peace and love. Now, with Marshall so bruised and helpless, the house a shambles of broken glass and debris, and the rest of us racked with demons of fear, I didn't care about whose case would be stronger before The Movement. It was suddenly clear that the opinions and loyalties of the underground editors meant nothing—mere politics and commerce. The important thing was that the people I loved, and their home, were being raped and slashed and defiled. Marshall was almost unconscious, Cathy was nearly mad, Steve Diamond was now getting a roughing-up, half of my Vermont household had been struck and threatened and vilified without even being "guilty" of the heist, and there was still no press to pacify them with; I feared my family would never recover from what had already happened and what lay in store, I feared the farm would be in ashes for us, I feared we could never rid ourselves of all the poison of the hour just past. I urged Marshall to give them the press and end this *Walpurgisnacht,* but he had seen the worst by then and was looking at it from the other side, and he would not relent.

By somebody's arbitrary choice, our group was then broken up and redistributed throughout the first floor of the house, each room being equipped with one or two stick- or knife-bearing guards at the door. I was in the front bedroom, where I was allowed to walk about so long as I did not leave or insult my guard. And from there I had an excellent view of the next chapter in the long evening: the arrival of Bill Lewis and Steve Marsden in the hydraulic truck. Neither our group nor the raiders knew for sure whether the press would be in the truck, but on the chance that it was, the Yorkers raced out of the house, the bushes, and their lookout posts along the road and tried to stop the truck by climbing its running boards and jumping in front of it. Bill Lewis saw the light and tried to keep going, heading straight for a clump of Marxists stationed in the glare of his headlights. I longed for him to make it, to roar out of the driveway and send the Yorkers fleeing in their highly conscious fear of the police, but the truck stalled to a stop as both he and Steve were dragged from the cab and beaten on the ground. Bill fought back but was outnumbered. Sure that these two must know the whereabouts of the press, and utterly defeated by Marshall's refusal to talk, the raiders began working over Bill and Steve, who claimed ignorance. Steve was brought into the house and dragged around, and up a staircase, by the hair on his head. Once again hysteria broke out and Tom the Nazi started up with his metal rod. Once again windowpanes were kicked in and screams rang through the night, and no neighbor heard. And finally the name of the elderly man and woman who were housing the press came out.

George went to the phone and had somebody reconnect it, then got the phone number of the couple who had the press, and called it. It was by then 3:00 or 3:30 A.M., so the lady was frightened and alarmed by the call, it was apparent. "Just a minute, Marshall Bloom has got something to tell you," George said into the receiver as he handed the phone to Marshall, who had been hustled into the room by a team of brawny longhairs. Marshall, who looked even worse now than when I had been separated from him at 1:30 or 2:00, at first said nothing. "Tell her to give us the press," he was told while one man wrenched his arm behind his back. He took the phone and very calmly, although in a faltering voice, told the lady that everything was all right, she should go back to bed now, and if anybody bothered her she should call the police. And hung up.

I thought this was surely the end of us, for I could see George and a few others going into a rage beyond words. But I misjudged the situation; for, while the Yorkers were screaming at the top of their lungs, they were no longer beating Marshall. Marshall had bested them. He was no longer afraid, if he ever had been, and they were clearly not going to get our faithful old press no matter what. All the cards had been played, the raid as well as the heist had done its damndest. The Yorkers were exhausted, some from destroying inanimate things, others from beating on people, all from running around all day Monday, driving north all night, and facing a long drive back again. They got a check for $6,000, the deed to the farm, and what seemed like enormous pleasure in brutal revenge. The check was canceled at 9:00 A.M., the deed was never worth anything, and their pleasure, like our pain, has surely waned with the passage of time. Add it up and you'll see: all you need is love!

And love, ironically, made its way into the evening. As I was curled up on the floor in the bedroom, waiting for dawn, I heard voices singing "Amazing Grace." I recognized Verandah's voice and the voice of the lead vocalist for The Children of God. Both factions were singing now, in mellifluous harmony. I could not believe what I heard.

Amazing grace
How sweet the sound
Could save a wretch like me.

It was a choir of angels singing to end a night of hell, and its lustiest members were evenly distributed between the executioners and the victims.

The water is wide,
I cannot pass o'er,
And neither have I wings to fly.
Build me a boat
That will carry two,
And both shall go, my love and I.

I cried to hear these beautiful sounds, so gentle and kind, made by brothers and sisters sitting all in a circle on the bare and blood-spotted floor. All that had happened in that house that night was not between rulers and subjects, police and people, but between allies in a struggle for justice and freedom. And I knew that the singing was no truce really, that the morning would bring new and greater antagonisms, that we could not yet forgive each other's trespasses and probably never join hands in cause together (as, indeed, we never really had), yet the music continued.

> *And before I'll be a slave*
> *I'll be buried in my grave*
> *And go home to my Lord and be freee!*

Well something has to be said for the human race, and that is: if you can mix among it without regard for pride and material gain, and you do not depend on anyone for your survival, you'll find it a noble race of living energy, a divine force, and wholly good.

The eternal verdant sunrise began then, and all the raiders slipped away before light of day could shine on us all together. No words were spoken, even among themselves, for they all seemed to take the dawn as their cue to leave. They left behind the trees and streams and peep frogs to help us in our revival. They left us broken and twisted and living in the aftermath of a bombing—that is, left us as they themselves had been left. We took from them the machinery with which they planned to voice their politics, and their politics are their identities; they took from us our blood, our energy, and whatever vision we had left of a "revolution" through new political ideas and action. Once their motors died off in the distance, the only noise to be heard in the big red farmhouse was Bob Dylan singing "It's All Over Now, Baby Blue."

III. Morning of the Great Beginning

Since LNS was to be published from the Montague farm, that is, since we couldn't conceive of life on the farm or anywhere else *without* LNS, steps had to be taken at once, our blurred and weary heads notwithstanding. That $6,000 check, it was agreed, must be canceled and the money returned to Cathy, who was our conduit for the news service; and if the check was to be canceled, then the entire raid with its assault and battery, grand larceny, and kidnapping had to be reported to the police. The press had to be gotten and LNS mailing Number 100 sent out immediately. Would there be no rest? We climbed into Steve Diamond's old station wagon (named Wilderbeast), John Wilton wisely declining to come along, and headed for the Turners Falls, Massachusetts, police station, where the officer in charge had a very, very hard time believing his ears, and many hours were consumed in getting the story down on paper so that the legal papers and the money could be reclaimed as legally stolen. There was only one policeman in Turners Falls that morning and his benign face and truly courtly behavior left me with the realization that the local cops could hardly have saved us from the midnight raiders, not only because they would be unable to distinguish the raiders from the victims ("an inter-hippy dispute," the afternoon papers said), but because their authority hangups were so much milder than the authority hangups of our New York brothers. From Turners Falls, we went to the courthouse in Greenfield, Massachusetts, where kidnapping complaints were issued against thirteen of the thirty raiders, that being the largest number we could identify, and assault complaints issued against two or three. It struck me that Montague farm was going to have an even tougher time getting "accepted" by its small-town, rural neighbors after they learned the circumstances in which it was born, but there we were in the courthouse, willingly dealing with judges and district attorneys and newspaper reporters—all of whom were strangely fresh and intelligent and none of whom showed signs of prejudice against us because of our appearance. It was certainly bizarre, but I felt these local enforcement people were my friends, which is to say not my enemies (cf. Thoreau). And we *did* have to establish our legal rights in order to avoid losing the money and the news service with it.

Have to, had to, have had to. We still operated in such terms in those dark days, just as most of you still do. We had to put out an issue of LNS every now and then; had to pay the piper for his tunes; had to register and file ourselves away for future goodies. My goal is to never have to do a damn thing for the rest of my life; and while many would call that immaturity, irresponsibility, or sloth, I call it FREEDOM. The motley assembly in the Greenfield courthouse that morning was anything but a gathering of free men, let me tell you.

Well, the big big trial on those kidnapping and assault charges didn't come up until October of 1968, but this book will end before then, so let me cheat on chronology a little and fill you in on the way this mini-adventure ended. The New York crowd, no fools themselves, went home and got themselves one of those lawyers the very cut of whose clothing gave him away as a city slicker—quite ridiculous he seemed in the baggy-pants atmosphere of the Greenfield court. But he got some kind of injunction against the six thousand dollars in the Amherst bank (although the check was deposited in the LNS account in New York, it never cleared), freezing it there so that neither faction could spend it until some nebulous trial-in-the-sky proved who was the real LNS. And do you know, friends, that goddamn money is *still* in the Amherst bank today and not one step closer to being freed, though it's been eaten away by bank and legal fees down to about $3,000 total. The Montagroovians decided some time ago that those breads had stale karma and they didn't want 'em anyway; and the New York crowd proposed giving them away to a third "revolutionary" group, but of course nobody has yet decided which lucky party will get the windfall. The New Yorkers never did sue or press the charges of "embezzlement" against the Virtuous Caucus, probably because we did, and still do, have legal title to the name of the news service.

When the trial of the New York Thirteen came up

in court, then, we finagled with lawyers and judges and generally gave the impression that, while we were certainly kidnapped that night, it was all blood under the dam and we weren't terribly anxious to press the charges. So, and to my astonishment, the court agreeably reduced the charges to disturbing the peace and everybody got $25 and $50 fines, good money thrown after bad but it's an old story in radical circles, those $50 fines. I sat in the back of the courtroom with my copy of Thoreau's *Week on the Concord and Merrimack Rivers* and engaged the bailiff in practical considerations about the relative pollution of different parts of the Merrimack, on which I was born and off which I skipped pebbles while but a lad.

*   *   *

Thus, on the morning of the great beginning, and after the dust had cleared, everything had changed and yet remained the same. Neither of the warring halves of LNS had a penny to its name, though both *thought* they had $6,000 (this clearly couldn't be true; for LNS to have more than $100 just lying around in some bank was too out of character); each party had a place to live and work, which required constant injections of money and goods to maintain; and there were all of a moment *two* distinct publications bearing the same name. This left a few people confused, but—we should have known—most people didn't really care. Most of the readers couldn't tell the difference between "LNS-NY" or "LNS-Mass." printed at the beginning of an article; and the underground and college editors used stories from both news services chosen on the basis of personal taste. As before, most of them neglected to pay their bills, although a few decided to send $7.50 a month to each of the LNS's. And on it went.

Members of each faction would meet again before August expired, now in Chicago at the Democratic Convention, or more properly *outside* the Democratic Convention. There, the midnight raid at Montague was reenacted a thousandfold, as police, politicians, detectives, National

Guard, and all came down hard on the new generation with their arsenal of fiendish weaponry, and the new style of demonstrator—the well-armed demonstrator, the screaming demonstrator, the contemptuous and bitter demonstrator—held sway over his older, olive-branch-bearing counterpart. Even being together in such a maelstrom of nightsticks and nerve gases did not bring Montague and New York people into the same family, and the competition for readers and income went on unceasingly.

But the morning of the great beginning held more in trust for the farm family than they could have known at that time. Whereas the Yorkers went back to Claremont Avenue, a familiar if desolate environment, to continue the routine they had established, the farm people were now in a wholly new and different world—a world in which the climate meant infinitely more than the local political situation, in which trees were for warmth in the winter and rivers for swimming in the summer, in which carpentry and husbandry and gardening became important skills directly related to their survival and nobody was available to perform services for them. The world at the farm was more concrete, earthly, practical, and real, less abstract, political, or commercial. Their world was no longer held up by stacks of paper and printed things, but by oak beams and maple planks.

While the (new) presses rolled relentlessly down in the Big Apple, Little Johnnie sat in a big cow barn in Massachusetts getting progressively less attention as the water system needed repair, the winter arrived, and the house and barn began to fill up with animals—first dogs and cats, then chickens, goats, pigs, a cow, and ducks. Little Johnnie's motor and gears grew rusty while the people paid mind to their failing VWs, their tractor, and their truck. LNS in Montague appeared twice a week, then weekly, then every two weeks, until Christmas came and it was twenty degrees below zero and Johnnie froze till spring. Weeks and then months passed, and nobody in the house could get it together to go out there and print up an issue of LNS, everybody had better and more useful things to do. So that by February of 1969, and without any kind of public notice to the subscribers or the readers, LNS in Montague quietly died.

There was a mourning period of who knows how many weeks or months during which Steve Diamond or Marshall Bloom would plaintively suggest that another issue of the news service be rolled off the press, but it never happened. And when the spring broke in 1969 and the long darkness of winter, the first winter, had been undeniably survived, there was no trace of LNS left in the place. LNS was a monstrous, repressive form of expression, a Franken-stein we had created but later disposed of, something very much in the past and good riddance to it. LNS was one of those things we had left behind when we came over to the New Age.

LNS lives in New York City now, which is the ap-propriate place for it. In spring of 1969, I paid a call on the Claremont Avenue office, where I found Allen Young, George Cavalletto, Sheila Ryan, and a crowd of newcomers whose names I did not learn. The office seemed the same as always, phones ringing and people rushing about attempt-ing to get this or that piece of information down in print. The Beatles, who had been quasi-heroes to us in Washing-ton, were denounced on the staff bulletin board as counter-revolutionary sellouts ("LNS Backs Stones in Ideological Rift with Beatles," a New York headline had actually read), and I had the feeling that in this special universe (called the New Left though it is as Old as history) every-thing—music, the planets, sex, love, *everything*—was seen in limited *political* terms. The news service was now striv-ing, it seemed to me, to represent the common people of America—"workers," even—and *mis*representing them as much as their senators and congressmen do; for just as the vote-getters in Washington act in their own behalf and not for the public interest, so does Liberation News Service es-pouse ideas and stand behind leaders which the general American public finds Communistic, heretical, and foul.

There, in the hustle-bustle atmosphere of radical activism, I wanted to scream, "There are no answers! there are no systems! this is not my salvation! leave me alone!"

Allen, George, and Sheila did not look well. It was clear they never saw sunlight, they were pale and flabby-looking. Those barred windows had been covered over with venetian blinds, and the door to the office was kept double-locked at all times, a peephole installed in it to assure that it was never opened for an unauthorized person. Inside, the office was lit by ribbons of fluorescent bulbs and ventilated by a few partially open windows. The LNS mailings themselves were full of accounts of this or that SDS council, convention, or meeting; "kill the pigs"; "students are workers" (that's a hot one); lives and heroic exploits of some North Korean general (general!), some Latin American guerrilla; quotes from this or that martyred revolutionary. Almost nothing about the place, the people there, or what they published had any sense of humor, for the world of political realities is grim and deathly, and they operate in that world to the exclusion of all others, at least during their "business hours."

Allen Young got Steve Diamond in a corner room and was discussing business—when would Marshall sign a paper giving the New York office legal title to the name of the news service? What was to become of the money in the Amherst bank? Intermittently, people darted in to speak of somebody's trial, somebody else's bust, the pigs versus the Panthers. The number of subscriptions to LNS had actually gone down, to slightly more than four hundred, Allen told me, but he remained optimistic about the caliber of the underground press and was of course faithfully working toward that big big revolution. The difference between Allen and me struck me in a phrase: he sees the revolution as "the people" all working together, I see it as the people all *not*-working together. He and LNS are "in the struggle" now, while I and Montague Farm are living the postrevolutionary life. LNS is now a reliably frequent, entirely businesslike publishing operation just like *Time* magazine, only from the other side of the fence; and I am an indigent dropout. I no longer have *any* kind of program to save the world, let alone nineteenth-century Marxism, except perhaps to pay attention to trees. I wish everybody would pay as much attention to trees as I do, but since everybody won't listen, I'll just go my solitary way and strive to enjoy what may well be the last days of this beautiful but deteriorating planet.

It was on the morning of the great beginning that the seed of all these heavy changes was sown, though we couldn't have been aware.

*   *   *

So long, Washington, good-bye New York. You were life and life only, I was a part of your teeming life. I didn't know any better, I went the road many others had traveled, and came through still healthy and ready, now, for heavier changes still. Fare thee well, Liberation News Service, new masters at your tired helm, and they too only temporary guardians of your well-being. An hour may be forever, tomorrow is another day, etc., etc. I'm sorry I didn't save the poor and hungry; now I am poor and hungry too (and such a career I could have had!) so I guess I've objectively made matters worse. I'm sorry I didn't put an end to war, but at least I haven't contributed to one of them. I'm sorry I didn't make all men brothers, but that's already a truth and maybe someday will be a fact as well. I tried my best, I really did, and now I'm walking that lonesome valley by myself, my dreams in lurid technicolor, but I'm still trying my best, giving it all I've got. It was grand knowing you, sorry to have to go, destiny calls me, head for the hills. Who knows what lies beyond them mountains? May all your Christmases be white and all your imperialist states crumble. Good night, brave spirits.

*   *   *

NOW CLOSE THE WINDOWS

Now close the windows and hush all the fields:
  If the trees must, let them silently toss;
No bird is singing now, and if there is,
  Be it my loss.

It will be long ere the marshes resume,
  It will be long ere the earliest bird:
So close the windows and not hear the wind,
  But see all wind-stirred.

Robert Frost, *A Boy's Will*

CHAPTER TEN

Afterwords: It's never really the end

I. Summer

Summer is Easy Street, anybody can live in summer. Boogers boogers boogers from New York and Boston, even Washington, come up here "for the summer." The days are so awfully long, vulgar almost, and when you're saying "that's enough, already," the sun is still hanging in there a full three feet off the curvature of the planet. Weed the potatoes in the morning if you can, it's too hot in afternoon and too many bugs at twilight (Skeetie-Bugs-Bite). Stretch the barbed-wire fence a few more feet, horse won't run through this one, give up and go to the beaver pond for a skinny-dip. Nice day for a drive, let's take one—easy to go anywhere in summer, just git up and do it. Talk about all the things to be done before fall, chimney cleaned, wood gathered, build this build that, new tires for the old car, radiator work on the tractor, insulate the shed. Waves of hot air and lush chlorophyll green everywhere.

Raspberries come first, just before strawberries, then a month later blueberries—no peaches till the fall. Who can ever tire of raspberries? You're stomping around in some picky bush and you think they're all gone but HERE'S a juicy one and there's a whole *clump* of 'em, take 'em home in a bucket and next week, at the latest, this field's gotta get *mowed*. Get rid of all this high grass, fun to lie down in and peek through the black-eyed susans at the farm in the valley, the only farm for miles, with its funny red barn and the only thing moving the tail on the mare. Barf-Barf the happy border collie, even, found shade under

191

the truck and Rosemary Goat is sleeping under the apple tree alongside Horse Simon's grave. Lovely high grass, but it's getting to be a jungle up here and gotta get mowed, so you can smell the blood of the cut blades of grass and milkweed floating in moving mist early mornings.

Summertime to find a new part of the woods— never been *here* before, maybe I'm lost, Barf-Barf lead the way!—and get all irate about the state the world is in. Time on your hands to worry about the government, ain't cold enough to bring you *real* problems. Summertime to take it like it comes, here today gone tomorrow, visit from old friends, write that novel, paint that picture, stage a play, send letters to somebody who can help stop all this Vietnam murder, go to the drive-in quadruple motorcycle feature. Motorcycle! Love dat motorcycle! Ride the bike, the horse, the tractor, or the car or just grin easy into the everlasting sun and *walk*. Stop for a drink from the bubbling stream. Neighbor's worried about boogers, gotta get an effective booger-control 'n protect our privacy. Well *I'm* a booger we're all boogers except for the Indians and I'm hardly never an Indian, only when I sleep in the grass by the campfire; but I see what you mean, Don, crazy New York boogers with their shiny useless automobiles, oughta leave 'em a big secret rut in the road, rip out their mufflers and make a roaring warning from two miles away—Beware the American Middle-Class Coming!

Summertime easy time in the house—newspapers call it a "commune," we never call it anything but home. Everybody home loves everybody else, plenty of room you see for the planet is open and friendly even in dark night, nobody gets in other guy's hair too bad. Then the lettuce comes, followed by spinach and squash and all those not-very-trippy vegetables, until August comes the TOMA-TOES O everybody loves tomatoes and CORN and that with berry pies, homemade bread, and maybe Marty 'n Connie even caught a fish makes a wunnerful meal. Keep the goat away from the onions!

Grow, grow, grow, it's summertime. Make a big food to last through the winter, the essential thing is love and survival without help from nobody, get strong, defend ourselves against the elements and the ugly world, make everything *grow*. It's warm, get some new chickens, bargain for a puppy, cats have kittens, population explosion. Everything grow, good sun shines upon us, gives us vitamins. We are life on a planet, that's the point—what are they doing to our planet? They are dumping shit in our fine clear streams, they are poisoning our foods, they are decimating our forests and using up our oxygen with their highways. Must grow vegetables, animals, and people to offset these disturbing obscenities. Encourage everybody to grow, show everybody what a beautiful planet we are part of. I worship the sun, I am glad to be here and now, I don't wanna move to no other planet. Play with the worms, the frogs, butterflies, moths, birds, bats, porcupines, woodchucks, fish, deer, cattle, owls, chickens, bobcats, dogs, cats, rabbits, raccoons, skunks, grasshoppers, fleas, moles, ants, and a thousand critters without names; and the milkweed, sycamore, maple, cherry, apple, elm, pine, and weeping willow; and the dandelions, begonias, tulips, lilacs, and goldenrods and morning glories. See how everything lives now on our planet, celebrate life!

Maybe it'll rain and Michael won't have to go haying, then it's a holiday! See how the beaver pond is clear and fresh after a big rain. Maybe it won't rain and the spring will run dry, hauling water to the chickens and the horse and what about bathing? Some nights it'll be so warm you could go out there stark naked, other nights so cold you want to start a fire. In August? Well a campfire will do really and it's warm under the covers so you can sleep. But if it rains, let's go down to Montague and help Marshall pick his cucumbers! The pickle company is getting bitchy and we can't afford to hire no braceros. Where indeed will we get next month's mortgage (well, Raymond's writing a book for Beacon Press, and they'll come through one of these days)? Can't afford no beer, the checking account has got seventy-two cents only, but Tom always has beer and maybe Don has some too. Dale reads a lot, it's summer, and Verandah is cutting pine shingles for her house won't be so cold *next* February! Let's be grasshoppers and not ants this time around, hey? But first—the beaver pond!

But summer is brief, here's September. Still pretty warm for September. There's me in the woods throwing elm logs down to Richard, logs that Laurie cut yesterday and we'd haul 'em too except the truck's caught in the orchard. Connie is wearing late goldenrods in her breast. It's Indian Summer, hey this is getting ridiculous it's supposed to be a cold climate. Everybody pitch in and we'll survive. Indian Summer can't last forever you know, though it threatens to. The old planet is still moving, the sun's getting further away, it's getting pitch-black darker sooner, and the kids in town are waiting in the hollow for the fat yellow bus to take them to school. But it's "No School All Schools All Day" as Superintendent Hennessey used to say (he's dead now) and there'll be no more teacher's dirty looks for this kid. Gotta survive and save the planet. The Indians bring us red and yellow lush peaches, juicy and ready to go, it's just like California! "Some one of these mornings," Don says, "we're going to wake up and find out it's

II. Fall

And the mountain fog is more like a frost these early mornings, and can it be? Come Verandah, come Laurie, come Elliot and Ellen and Richard, and tell me the old maples haven't dropped acid! Where all was green for the long lazy days is flaming lurid yellow and red and brown! The world is red! You remember that oak, why only yesterday it was just a little brownish and now it's it's CANARY YELLOW. Hey, I'm cold, I'm gonna get a sweater, be back in a minute O K?

O now there is not a moment to waste, there is still not enough wood and how can we ever finish building the loft? Don't worry, Laurie says (and Laurie knows all about this stuff), fall is the best time to build. Get the last of the food in, it's October now, make the house ready for the big bad winter, hear the chain saw busy in the forest all day now, troop through the fields carrying logs, up on the roof chain-cleaning the old chimney, saving newspapers to start the fire, hammer and nails and shingles against the growing wind. "Well it sure ain't Washington," that one is good for a laugh. "Everybody come outside, quick, come outside." Laurie is dancing on his hobnailed boots. And a whole family of honking Canadian geese is flying V-formation (V for victory, Vietnam, Verandah, and Vermont) right over the barn and once again saying so long! God they are splendid creatures, hope they don't pass over some hunting boogers in Connecticut!

Hunters come. Many of them, in their bright red jackets, riding in squadrons in the backs of pickup trucks, and walking in groups down the frostbitten road at dawn. Shots ring out everywhere, they sound like twigs cracking under your foot. There is deer to be had in those woods, some want it for sustenance but most just for sport. The newspaper says there are fewer hunters every year, the popularity of it is declining, well that's good, but it's little consolation to the mother of the seventeen-year-old son always lying dead in October, or to the people and animals forced to stay home while the land becomes a battleground.

But enough, home has its joys too. Lengthy checker games by firelight. Good books. Frost on the pumpkin. Noodle comes home on Hallowe'en after being given up for dead, on the same day the new 1949 tractor almost falls into the brook. O that Mother Honeywell, eighteenth-century witch, got her designs on us!

Jack and Sarah come on a nippy October Sunday, it was a little cold in Boston but it's snowing like hell, a ferocious blizzard, in Vermont, and their helpless Buick gets stuck on the road. It's crazy and wonderful to see snow in October but we're not ready yet, if winter's here we are doomed. Relax, Laurie says winter is not here yet. The FBI come to the farm, too, all the way from New York State, but I am in the woods and they can't ask me a few questions. When they return, they are astounded at where I live, but of course they don't understand, I offer them hot chocolate but no thanks.

All the leaves fall and all the grass is dead; gone the bugs and birds and endless sunshine. Help, our planet is dying! Thanksgiving is red corncobs, white wine, mashed potatoes and turnips, and turkey with stuffing. We're not vegetarians by choice, only by economic reality. Gus and Martha come, and Frankie their son of the New England string quartet. Laurie plays the grand piano and Elliot plays Dylan; Marty is already charting next year's garden and Verandah is dreaming of twins in Gemini. But Gus is a medical practitioner, a physician, and that comes in handy when a group of strange strangers on horseback arrives to offer Thanksgiving howdies and announces that there is a girl in labor pains in their house at that moment. Thanksgiving evening, little Carpenter is born on the green river and The Baby Farm gets its name. Hey, don't play, the wind is beginning to howl.

Cold and dark November days begin to look blue and there is evil in the air. Sometimes groups of people come from the cities and want to build a shack, settle down, they won't bother us in the least, can't they stay and double the population? No, you can't stay, go do it yourself, don't suck energy off our trip, go away, ten's comfortable but twenty's a crowd and soon it'd be fifty and we'd have all the congestion griefs we're seeking to escape. Go do it yourself, I tell them, thousands are doing it, and more to come, and it's exploding all over, the united refugee states of Vermont and New Mexico being most obvious. But I always feel deep-down rotten when I tell 'em to go away.

The thin film of frost turns to snow, first just an inch or two, then deep so you fall through it and come crashing down on bended knee. Lucky Barf-Barf has a warm coat and sleeps in the snowbanks without a chill. Get the furnace higher now, winter's coming on. Do I have to shit in the outhouse? Of course silly it's thirty dollars to have the honey bucket sucked empty once it's full and now the man from town won't do, says the shit will freeze in his truck on its way through the hollow. Man who go to the city to see old friends take plenty shits and showers while there. But it's still not all over till it's the equinox, the shortest day, and then Christmas, when the green tree glistens with popcorn and tinsel, it's thirty degrees below zero with a bucking fifty-mile-per-hour wind and you know it's

III. Winter

The life of the community, the families building their new nation, is the only life on the planet now. Outside the door is adventure and beauty beyond description, but also danger. The dead bodies of our predecessors were stored in the barns till spring thawed out the land. Now the community can pray together for survival, and test its skills against the wild wrath of the heavens. Now the ladies will sew and the gentlemen throw logs into the throbbing furnace. And when one of our number is away, and days have passed since his or her return, we will all chafe and fret together for a safe and happy ending to the absence, a joyous homecoming. Now, too, much time will be "wasted" in endless conversations and exhausting efforts to keep the car and jeep running, and all to no progress, but merely holding the status quo.

Winter is a hard time if only because utter sloth is out of the question. Keep ahead of it, don't let it get you. But winter invites us to intellectual warmth, let us puzzle this or that out together, let's consider the hows and whys of this country, this world, in this time. There is time, the winter is long; there is time for the first time in our lives. What a luxury to have time!

One bracing sharp morning, it is a holiday. The road's not plowed, so there's nowhere to go. There's Michael and I walking down to Don's with a child's sled trailing behind us. The telephone wires, which do not stop at our house, are singing a happy tone; Michael tells me, and I believe it, that it is the ladies of town yakking to their friends that makes the strange noise. Actually it is the ice-locked wires vibrating in the cold wind, backed by the telephone pole which quivers in percussion. Tom's old maple trees speak from the dead in awesome croaks. Michael and I climb on our sled, pull down our knit caps over our heads, and off through the woods we go, cutting through the cleanest zero-degree air in the world and swooshing around seven-foot-high snowbanks with WHOOEEs galore. Don's wife Phoebe makes us coffee while his dog Daisy fans the fire with her tail.

On another day, fire breaks out . in the chimney. One and all must haul the water in buckets and bottles to the roof, which is quickly a sheet of smooth ice. We are our own fire department that night, but after the job is finished in dark and cold, and the danger passed, the house is frozen too and the furnace cannot be reignited. Fire is our god, fire is a microcosm of the sun. All you need is love and fire—one for the soul, the other for the body. Beware when either expires.

Maple flows in February and March. Marty once again to the rescue, with buckets and spigots to catch the precious sap. Pancakes may be fashioned of simple grains, none of your Aunt Jemima bullshit, and with the syrup makes a fantastic breakfast. That's Connie starting the peppers and tomatoes in an improvised greenhouse with electric bulbs for sun. March comes in like a lion, goes out like the Aurora Borealis, brilliant red northern lights, like the end of the world or something. Will wonders never cease?

AN ARIA FOR WINTER & *THE LADY FROM OKLAHOMA*

Wind caught in nets	*When the heavens opened like an* *Easter egg*
Wind piped through lungs of the woods like tuberculo- sis	*and the sun fell out* *with a yolk of broken prom-* *ises*
Birds huddled in their wings like overcoats	*a lady came by Greyhound* *from Oklahoma*
Wind snapping the arms from the orchard	*with a bird-brain like a* *homing pigeon* *looking for her man,* *and had we seen him,*
earth hidden in its snow skin like a baked potato	*Oh, that bull-in-a-china-* *shop-worn take-your-* *chance man* *juggled her heart*
wild cat frozen eating a robin, ice with teeth,	*and fiddled his way* *toward Mexico,* *where*
lockjaws of the wind,	*they clapped the scofflaw* *in a bandit's cell*
white mountains, a prison in winter, Gatekeeper of the wind	*for crimes unrelated to* *season* *or the lady* *who is shaking in her boots* *by the stove*

who is our master,

who will not take bread &
*   soup*
at our table

shelter the lady

who babbles her story
like a schoolgirl with a gold
*   star.*

Black peach clinging to the
snow tree

I have come and I have
*   gone*

like a fetus

from Oklahoma

Deer will not eat it

where my father

though they are taut with
    hunger

is king of the rodeo,
where I was his gypsy—

wander on tiptoe

cowgirl majorette

Wind bellowing across the
    pasture
like a superhighway

I have traveled the map o'
*   mundi,*
oceans, islands,
highways like snakes or
*   arteries,*

snow seeds glinting in
the evening sun
like dust.

and in the whole world
there is one face
on one man

Lockjaws of the wind
at nightfall

who split my heart
like a walnut
with his squirrel teeth

Wind trapped in a cage
of stars

who nibbled the tenderest
*   part*
until it was gone

Wind caught in nets   *I wear the shell*
                                   like a locket
                                   sang the lady from
                                      Oklahoma.

                                                    Verandah Porche

     The community, in striving to be free and create a
living, peaceful alternative, has set itself the winter as its
great test. "The whole world is watching." Here's the beginning of the "peace movement" of the 1970s, here's a
clumsy attempt at self-sufficiency, here's a bigger underground press than ever, for each hath one and is one. The
word is spreading faster than wind could carry it. What are
you waiting for?
     The community survives. The first patch of planet
turns up brown and grisly, but something other than white!
After a dozen false starts, we get together and call it

IV. Spring

     When the green is not thick and dazzling, but
remarkably frail and wispy, almost threatens to die again
before it can really blossom. I skip up to the orchard on
prematurely bare feet. Violins are playing a delicate air.
Doors and windows are flung open, rugs beat, all that
stuffy karma chased away—and here's Bob Dylan again
with "Nashville Skyline" ("love that country pie!") to
accompany the bluebirds outside my window. Laurie says
let's have a May Day and invite all the communards from
this part of Vermont and Massachusetts too, and by God
it's a huge Hobbit convention! Flutes, guitars, flags, tam-
bourines, costumes, bonfires, and fertility rites! "Out-a-
site," as my Baby Farm friends would say. Marty and Connie caught a trout! Steve Diamond announces he is to
father a son and call him Tree! Every new flower gets a
crowd of admirers.

It's hard to keep from smiling, though you wouldn't want to anyway. Smile, it's spring! Kiss your neighbor, it's time for more building, new planting, new and more ambitious projects than ever—everything from a New Age library building to movies and books and babies! Let us now then cease with our complaining about the state the world is in, and make it *better*. We're not trying to convince the world—the world has an energy of its own, and we're only a tiny part of that. We're only trying to change ourselves, what a preoccupation! But if we get better, if I get better, that's tangible change, isn't it?

❊   ❊   ❊

Begun in the darkness of December, 1968, finished on a blessed star-lit night in August, 1969. Planet died and reborn in interim. Truth everywhere if you but look for it. Good news under the sun and moon. Author a bit of a hermit, but reasonably communicative in small groups. "If you don't smoke, don't start." Best things in life still free. Though we'll probably never meet, dear friend, *I'm* with *you*.